The Complete Book of
BUDGERIGARS

The Complete Book

DEDICATION

This book is dedicated to the most willing helper of all, my wife Ronnie. Without her inspiration and confidence in my ability, the following pages never would have unfolded.

A flock of wild budgerigars converge mid-stream on a mud bank to bathe and drink.

# of BUDGERIGARS

JOHN SCOBLE

BLANDFORD PRESS
POOLE   DORSET

ACKNOWLEDGEMENTS

I wish to acknowledge with gratitude the valuable suggestions and help I received from my editor Anne Lawrence. High praise must also be given to the photographer Ray Joyce for his unlimited patience with difficult subjects. My grateful thanks to Norm Rastall who helped me on numerous occasions with my problems. I am indebted to a great many contributors and of these I particularly wish to thank Bill Cooper, Bill Dunbier and Vic Pitt. My warmest thanks must go to Ray Kramer for his confidence in promoting me for the writing of this book.

Photographs for this book were taken by *Ray Joyce* and the *author*. Other photographic contributions are gratefully acknowledged from:
Dacre Stubbs
The Mitchell Library
The Australian Museum
B. Hutchins
Michael Morcombe
The Australian Information Service
J. Balls. U.K.
The Budgerigar Council of Australia

Designed by Willy Richards

First published 1981 by Lansdowne Press, Sydney, a division of RPLA Pty Ltd

© Copyright John Scoble 1981

First published in UK 1982 by Blandford Press, Link House, West Street, Poole, Dorset
2nd Impression 1982
ISBN 0 7137 1262 7

Typeset in Australia by S.A. Typecentre Pty Ltd, Adelaide
Printed by Koon Wah Printing Pte. Ltd.

CONTENTS

*This wild green budgerigar shows the bright colour and
attractive appearance which have made the budgerigar the
world's most popular caged bird. All budgerigar colours have
evolved from this wild green species.*

Photographs for this book were taken by *Ray Joyce* and the *author*. Other photographic contributions are gratefully acknowledged from:

Dacre Stubbs
The Mitchell Library
The Australian Museum
B. Hutchins
Michael Morcombe
The Australian Information Service
J. Balls. U.K.
The Budgerigar Council of Australia

FOREWORD

This is a wonderful and well-written book on our great hobby of budgerigar keeping and breeding, and will fill a huge gap, nothing like this has ever been available. This in itself is a credit to the author.

I have known John Scoble for a number of years, and in letters and conversation in my home he has proved that he is a very knowledgeable breeder, exhibitor and judge. The fact that he has also been able to study and see this fascinating little bird of ours in its wild state I found of great interest, even though I have been breeding and exhibiting the budgerigar for over 50 years.

It is written in terms that are easy for the beginner to our hobby to understand, especially the things that used to seem so complicated such as sex linkage and colour reproduction. For the more experienced fancier it will become a good reference book. No previous book has gone into so much detail on the bird and its make-up, and I am sure that many champions of longstanding will read items that they have never known before.

The many photographs, in colour and black and white, showing the wild birds in comparison with the exhibition stock, and the feathers from both types are also a new and interesting feature.

Every aspect of the hobby has been fully covered, down to the smallest detail, and John must be congratulated on the many hours he must have spent on research to bring this great book in to being.

Alf Ormerod
England.

Alf Ormerod is England's top breeder of budgerigars. He is also a much sought after judge for competitions in America and Europe.

PREFACE

This book is aimed primarily at the person who keeps budgerigars as a hobby. Regardless of the number of birds owned, he or she will soon come to appreciate some of the pleasures involved in the keeping of this small parakeet.

My first experiences with budgerigars date back to my childhood in Dubbo, New South Wales. We called them 'love birds' in those days and I remember trying to rob their nests in a large box tree but, fortunately for them, finding that they were too far down the trunk for my hand to reach. Then, in later years, while working on properties in far western New South Wales and Queensland, I used to observe them sometimes flying in groups. More recently, on a trip to the Northern Territory in 1974, I saw the most I have ever seen in their wild state.

It was shortly after arriving in Sydney, where I now live, that I became interested in the breeding of budgerigars for exhibition. That was twenty-five years ago and since then I have bred, and shown with success, almost every variety of budgerigar. I was fortunate enough during my early years in the hobby to be shown many breeding techniques by gifted people and I find that many of these techniques remain unsurpassed even today.

In addition, on four occasions in the last five years I have visited England where I have participated as a guest speaker at budgerigar meetings. While on these visits, I also had the privilege of conversing with many breeders, and looking at their birds and aviaries. Some of these breeders are recognised as being the best in the world.

Thus, over the years a great store of information has been given to me by many such people. To some it may be of little interest, but to others it represents a wealth of knowledge. Certainly much of this information has never been recorded and it is common knowledge that priceless records, written over a lifetime in the hobby, have often ended up being discarded and lost forever.

Since becoming involved in the writing of this book I have received even further information from people in all walks of life. No author could truly claim that all the subject matter covered in a book such as this was entirely his or her own: it is, rather, a subconscious accumulation of the author's and other people's ideas. Consequently my own personal reward in the writing of this book will be to see the thoughts and achievements of a great many people at last recorded.

AUTHOR'S NOTE

These writings represent an attempt by the author to encourage the fancier to approach the hobby in an innovative fashion, remembering always that the budgerigar is a member of the parrot family and that its real habitat is the inland of Australia where it existed for thousands of years and continues to exist in sometimes harsh conditions. Thus, in contrast to the canary which has been bred in captivity since the sixteenth century it is a relative newcomer to the pet scene and the budgerigar fancier can learn much from the canary culture, to which the same laws of inheritance and principles of selection and breeding apply.

Since the discovery of the budgerigar as a popular pet in the nineteenth century enormous strides have been made by breeders in developing new varieties and colours. While the majority of breeders will continue to breed for colour, others will attempt to produce new colours and with the appearance of every new mutation enormous interest will be created. At this time it is almost impossible to foresee what these new developments might be. Meanwhile, it is hoped, that the help, criticism and advice that may emerge after the reading of this book will have the effect of helping to define the goals and future development of this gregarious little parrot.

INTRODUCTION

The need for more information on the budgerigar is ever-increasing. One hundred and twenty-five years have passed since the breeding of budgerigars in captivity was first reported to take place in Berlin in 1855. Considering the numbers of budgerigars kept all over the world in captivity, from the household pet to the aviculturist, their numbers must be enormous. This evident popularity is reflected in the pet trade, which has become big business — supplying both the birds and the material required for their keeping. As a result of this demand bird farms have been established in some countries in order to facilitate a steady supply of budgerigars: these farms originated in Toulouse as long ago as 1880.

The exhibition budgerigar has also gained in popularity and there are many budgerigar societies throughout the world which have notable figures as their patrons. These specialist or mixed clubs exist to promote the budgerigar and facilitate the goodwill enjoyed by their many fancier members: they welcome new members.

The budgerigar could often be regarded as having a diplomatic effect. For example, if one is having a conversation with another person and it is disclosed you both have an association with budgies, the foremost topic of discussion will become the budgerigar.

Unfortunately, developments in veterinary science have not been as rapid as the growth in popularity of the budgerigar and the only comprehensive book on budgerigars written and compiled by an Australian was in 1933. The author was Neville Cayley[*1]. Cayley was fortunate enough to have had the co-operation of the top aviculturists of the times but, nevertheless, today a portion of his very interesting work has become out-of-date. Most of the remaining available literature has been written by authors living in the northern hemisphere and although much of their information is applicable to the breeding and keeping of the budgerigar in Australia, our seasons are directly opposite and our climate is vastly different. In addition, we have mutations in Australia that are either not found anywhere else in the world or vary from their overseas counterparts. This includes, of course, the native, wild budgerigar. Although very little research has been carried out on the nomadic habits of these birds, it has been possible to include some very interesting information resulting from recent investigatory work. The results of this research have important implications for the breeder of budgerigars and a theme that will be developed in the following chapters is that the closer we keep to nature in our treatment of cage birds the better the results.

Another essential feature in this book is the explanation of breeding. The genetic and colour reproductions are compiled as simply as possible and diagrams are used to enable the reader to see what results may be obtained from certain pairings. From a study of the genetic make-up of budgerigars it will become clear to the reader why they have intrigued those biologists and students who have used them for the study of genetics.

A colourful aviary line-up.

When a budgerigar is owned by a family it seems to become more attached to a child, as this pet has.

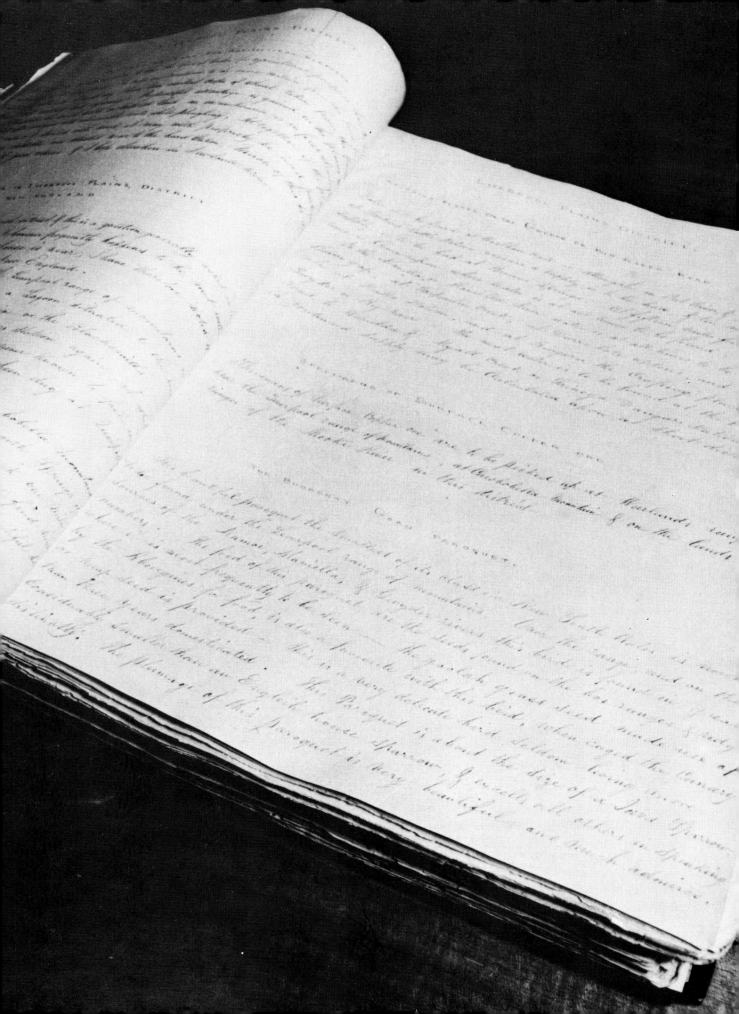

1 EARLY REFERENCE TO THE WILD BUDGERIGAR

The beautiful native parakeet, universally known as the budgerigar, is only one of the many unique species of animal and bird life that have evolved on the Australian continent. Like many Australian birds and animals its name was derived from that given to it by the Aboriginals who were living on the East coast at the time of the arrival of the Europeans. In general, the Aboriginal names for the budgerigar referred to its value as a source of food.

The earliest known illustration of a budgerigar, by Shaw and Nodder, was published in the *Naturalists Miscellany* in 1805. In this edition it was also given the scientific name of *Psittacus Undulatus*. (*Psittacus* — parrot; undulatus — diversified with waves.) Later, John Gould, the famous naturalist, added the generic name, *Melo*, meaning song, thus giving the budgerigar the name by which we know it today, *Melopsittacus undulatus*. This name refers to the common green bird seen in the wild. Some subspecies, representing only slight variations are: *M. undulatus intermedius*, which inhabits the Northern Territory and has paler colouration on its back and neck; and *M. undulatus pallidiciceps*, which inhabits Western Australia and is also paler, particularly on the head.

The following document (File No S6-1267) was found in the New South Wales Lands Department in Sydney in 1960 by an old fancier and friend, Mr Fred Hoare, who then suspected that it was one of the earliest documents written referring to the budgerigar. The writer, William Gardner, came to the colony from Scotland in the early days of settlement. He was employed as a teacher by the squatters in the New England district where, apparently, the budgerigar abounded. Notes written by him and now held by the Mitchell Library were written from 1830-1852.

In it, William Gardner uses the name *Budgerry Gaan*, and it seems that this is the first mention of a name which bears any resemblance to the name, budgerigar, as it is known today. Prior to this the budgerigar was referred to as, among other things,

the Undulated Parakeet, Shell Parrot and Zebra Parrot. Apparently, too, Gardner's letter was not known when Tom Iredale, Australian Museum Zoologist, and G. P. Whitley, Curator of Fishes at the Museum, unfolded their history of the earliest uses and variations of the name, budgerigar. The remarkable story of their search appeared in the Australian Museum's magazine, *Australian Natural History*, September 1962, pp 99-102.

The search began after Iredale and Whitley discovered in the archives of the Australian Museum what they believed was the earliest use of the term, The reference was contained in a book entitled, *Souvenirs d'un Voyage à Sydney (Nouvelle-Hollande) fait pendant l'année 1845*, which was written by a Frenchman, Benjamin Delessert, and was published in Paris in 1847. In it he describes a visit to a curio shop in Hunter Street, Sydney. The shop was owned by John Roach, who had come to Australia as a convict in 1833, and was an excellent taxidermist with birds, a skill which had proved extremely useful in the new colony because, as the investigators found in their historical search, John Roach was one of the earliest employees of the Australian Museum.

It seems that a visit to John Roach's shop was a must for the visitor to Sydney for there one could see 'all at once a selection of the animals found in New South Wales', presumably, stuffed. Nevertheless, it was a living creature that caught Delessert's eye and won his heart. He writes,

> But the parakeet which is the tiniest, rarest, and consequently the favourite, is the one called budgerry. It is the size of a canary, clear leaf-green in colour and striped with black on the back. Nothing is more amusing than to hear it chatter and ask for a piece of bread. It is a bird which can be taught without too much trouble.

Iredale and Whitley's search was to take three years to complete. Not only were they able to shed

An early reference from William Gardner's manuscript, describing the Budgerry Gaan and the Liverpool Plains, an area where John Gould recorded his observations of these small parrots.

673

****

GENERIC

Bill hooked : upper n
Nostrils round, place
Tongue fleshy, broad,
Legs short : feet scans

SPECIFIC C

Long-tailed green P.
  above with brow
  with blue spots,
  low at the base.

The highly elegant sp
on the present plate in it
of New Holland, and se
described. The upper
bill to the rump, are of
tifully crossed by numer
which become gradually
back and shoulders : the
pale olive-yellow edges :
together with the rump,
the throat pale yellow,
few small deep blue scat

MELOPSITTACUS UNDULATUS.

*This illustration by John Gould represents an old and a young bird feeding on grass. '**Birds of Australia**' vol v. p44. 1840*

*The early published illustration and description of the budgerigar – from Shaw and Nodder '**Naturalists' Miscellany**' pp673–674. 1805*

some light on the career of the 'rascally' John Roach, but they were also successful in tracing the history of the spellings of the names of this fascinating little bird. A summary of their investigations, which drew on the work of Percy A. Gilbert, W. A. Sanford and Robert Austin, is presented in the table below. Also included is the find of Fred Hoare, William Gardner's letter, which we must now regard as the very first recorded use of a variant of the name, budgerigar, as it is known today.

1830 Budgerry Gaan, Gardner

1845 Budgerry, Delessert

1847 Betshiregah, Leichhardt

1848 Betcherrygah, Gould

1849 Bidgerigung, Sturt

1850 Bougirigard, Huxley

1855 Budgerager, Bugeirigar, Austin and Sandford

A later reference to the Budgerry Gaan from the manuscript of William Gardner.

1861 Budgere Gar, Wheelwright

1870 Budgerigar, accepted modern spelling, Cassell's *Household Guide*

1889 Budjerigar. Newton *Dictionary of Birds*, 1893
Budgerrygar of standard works and check-lists
Budgerygah
Budgerigah
Budgerigar in an American publication
Budgerrgah

1896 Beauregard, Newton, 1896 (*Dict. Birds*, p.59)
Betcherygah
Boodgeree-gar
Budgee, Budgie (newspaper articles and vulgar speech)

1900 Budgereegah, Webster

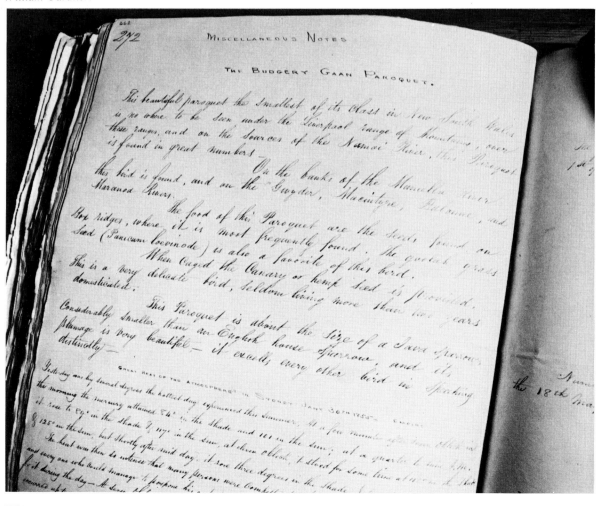

2 THE BUDGERIGAR AND ITS NATURAL ENVIRONMENT

One purpose of this book is to provide a detailed picture of the habits and life-style of the wild budgerigar. To accomplish this satisfying task I will have to rely heavily on recorded information, some of which is the result of work on scientific research programmes by academics. In addition, there are the observations of the layperson which are often recorded in newspapers. To all these people we are indebted — for without them, there would be very little interesting information available.

Many Australians and visitors to Australia may have had their first glimpse of a wild budgerigar while touring the inland. Perhaps while visiting the Flinders Ranges in South Australia where budgerigars seem to abound; or, while walking around the 9 km (5½ mile) base of the famous landmark of the Centre, Ayers Rock, they have seen them drinking at the many rock pools. If you have had the opportunity to observe them, flying in large or small flocks, you will have noticed they are great company fliers — continually wheeling and turning with the utmost precision, their rumps glistening vividly in the sunlight. Alternatively, you may have had the unique opportunity of seeing them, in thousands, crowded together on one or two dead trees near a source of water. At this first glimpse one is always surprised at how small the wild budgerigars are compared with their domesticated counterpart for contrary to the latter, their size never seems to vary.

The budgerigar is one of the smallest members of the Australian parrot family and is generally found throughout the Australian inland. Only rarely have they been known to venture near the coastal areas and only then in extreme drought conditions. Reports that they are migratory birds are incorrect as they live a completely nomadic existence — not unlike the tribal Aboriginal, with whom they have existed in harmony for many millennia. Like the Aboriginals, they have been governed in their movement by the availability of food and water.

An example of this co-existence is elaborated on by Professor Donald Thomson, who spent some time living with the Bindibus, a tribe of Aboriginals living in the Great Sandy Desert in Western Australia. This tribe used a throwing stick, called a *kul'o*, to kill birds when a flock came to waterholes to drink or descended to eat the seeds of the spinifex in the evening. Sometimes these hunters were able to bring in armfuls of dead or wounded birds and these were then prepared for eating.

The cooking or preparation of these kilkindjarri (budgerigars) was an eye-opener to the white man, accustomed to the waste involved in the preparation of poultry and larger game.

For the Bindibu can afford to waste nothing.

The birds were thrown on to the ashes of the small cooking fires and the feathers singed off, after which they were brushed and this process repeated until the bodies of the birds were free of feathers.

The whole of the bodies were eaten, including the bones, even the skull and brains.

The bill was set aside with certain other parts that were to receive special attention later.

The horny layer, yellow or orange in colour, which formed the outer covering of the bill, was then stripped off and discarded, the bill itself being eaten with the whole of the skeleton of the bird except the carina, or breast bone.

Even the viscera were picked over, and most of these eaten.

I cannot say that the people always eat almost the entire skeleton of these small parrots, but at this time they were hungry for *kuk'a* — for animal protein.[1]

When wild grass seeds were plentiful nets were also used by these clever hunters to capture birds, especially the budgerigars. The women usually made these from carefully selected reeds, strong silky grasses or bark from certain trees. These materials had to be soaked and pounded and then split into strands so that they could be plaited into a

Budgerigars watering along a tree-lined watercourse in western N.S.W.

strong, yet pliable, net. Often, the nets were then strung together to make one big net. With the aid of an interwoven vine used for a rope, this was strung between two trees across a narrow tree-lined watercourse, a short distance from some favourite roosting trees. Shortly before first light the men, women and children would place themselves in position. Curdling yells and shouts would break the silence and throwing sticks would be hurled into the trees. The birds would take off in a panic and be driven by the noise into the net. In the same fashion the nets could also be used at water holes where flocks came to drink.

In good seasons, when budgerigars were nesting, the collecting of youngsters to eat was often left to the Aboriginal children. They could climb a tree until they reached the knot hole and by thrusting a long pointed stick down into the nest hollow, retrieve an impaled youngster. Or, when there were nests in hollow logs, an even simpler task was to just rake them out with a stick.

When gathering food, the Aboriginals only collected what was required and there was no evidence of any destruction of the environment or species of bird or animal. In contrast, the arrival of European settlement and the introduction of the

Daybreak at Ayers Rock. The lush growth indicates a good season. The Olgas are in the background.

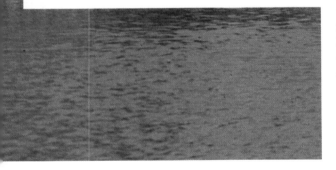

Wild budgerigars assembling on a tree in an arid area of South Australia.

The word 'desert' is a little misleading, even the Simpson Desert, one of the driest regions of Australia, which covers an approximate area of 80 000 sq km (50 000 sq. miles), sustains vegetation and animal life. A report on budgerigar sightings in the Simpson Desert in 1974 stated,

On the crossing, seen almost daily from 124 km west of Birdsville to Andado (approx. 1 000 km), singly or in parties up to twenty; none from Mulligan R. to Indianna; from there along Hale R. to Andado irregular. Mr. O. Fletcher in notes supplied to H. T. Condon (1946) said that 'one of the birds noted daily in the desert was the budgerigar'. The Madigan Expedition waited ten years for a good season because they crossed the desert on camels. Madigan (1945) reported that 'between Kalliduwarry and Annadale Homestead hundreds of budgerigars were nesting in hollow trunks of box gums'. Presumably, budgerigars range over the whole desert during favourable seasons.[2]

It was almost a century after the landing of Captain Cook in Botany Bay before the early explorers ventured into the interior and much of the country on the western seaboard has only been traversed in the last fifty years. Even today, much of it is still impenetrable and the landscape is dominated by arid landforms — small mountain ranges, rocky outcrops, and sandy ridges surrounded by predominantly flat, and mostly red sandy soil. Much of this area is sparsely covered with seeding spinifex hummocks, desert grasses and scattered areas of saltbush, together with stunted or low-growing bushes. In better watered country there is an abundance of native millets and many other seeding and succulent grasses as well as large desert oaks and mulga scrub, and around tree-lined watercourses many types of eucalypt grow. After unseasonal rain the landscape comes to life and appears for a time like a Garden of Eden, but, this is a thirsty land, and the colours are soon changed to brown.

Rainfall is irregular and unpredictable, averaging only 75 mm (3 in.) in some areas and falling mainly in spring and summer storms. This, combined with the high rate of evaporation, means that for most of the year the region is devoid of any surface water other than inland lakes, rock pools and springs because most rivers are seasonal and only flow for short periods in the wet season. For the most part,

feral cat and rabbit were to have a detrimental effect on the ecology of all bird life in Australia.

Between 1928 and 1949 rare sightings of budgerigar flocks were made in Adelaide, in close proximity to Melbourne, and even in the vicinity of the Myall Lakes (mid north coast of New South Wales). Today, however, their range is associated with the great inland grass areas in the arid (desert, semi-desert) and semi-arid (pastural or grazing areas) habitats, that is, about seventy per cent of the continent although, unfortunately, in many semi-arid regions, sightings of budgerigars, in reduced numbers, are now made at longer intervals.

they are only a network of waterholes and in long dry spells they may dry up altogether.

An additional source of water for the native fauna in more recent times is provided by the many bores which have been sunk to tap the saline water of the huge underground artesian basin. Despite its salinity the water is suitable for watering stock although it has been shown that budgerigars that drink this water do have an increase in their liquid intake.

Nevertheless, one wonders how the budgerigar manages to survive in the desert areas. Recent research has shown that the species has adapted to this environment and can survive on a minimum intake of water. It seems to have special abilities to withstand dehydration when the intake of water ceases altogether. Researchers experimenting with ten domesticated budgerigars found that,

When deprived of all water, Budgerigahs can exist with little weight loss for at least 38 days at an average air temperature of 30°C and average relative humidity of about 30 per cent, and at 20°C some individuals can apparently survive indefinitely without water. Two birds were still in good health after 130 days without drinking'.[3]

The results of this important research by T. J. Cade and J. A. Dybas Jr on the water economy of the bird supports the contention that it was possible for the large shipments of budgerigars to be transported to Europe from Australia without water during the nineteenth century. They also put paid to the misconception that all birds in the wild do not drink. Like all seed-eating birds the budgerigar must drink or get moisture from succulent vegetation or dew-laden grasses and tree leaves. In winter when the temperature varies from 26.7°C (80°F) during the day to −1°C (30°F) at night the budgerigar is able to survive without surface water by extracting the juices from the stems and leaves of plants and bushes and by taking the dew that forms on grasses, plants and the leaves of trees on the cloudless, still nights. In the extreme summer temperatures which average 38°C (100°F), they can conserve the moisture in their bodies by resting among the leaves of trees which release a cooling vapour.

Movements

Budgerigars are gregarious and are rarely seen in small numbers. Their flocks range in size from twenty to one hundred birds and numerous small groups often amalgamate in the air while flying to and from feeding and watering points. Similarly, when food and water supplies are low, due mainly to very dry conditions, budgerigars will begin to gather in one area. There, out of a sense of survival, separate flocks will merge into one great concourse numbering millions, appearing like clouds at times and actually darkening the sky as they fly en masse to new feeding and breeding grounds. Such flights have been reported as occurring at night as well as during the day; for example, in 1962 it was reported,

Bush Wireless — Alice Springs phoned yesterday to report that, towards dusk a week before, Mr and Mrs Ian Barton (of Phillip Creek near Tennant Creek) were motoring 'up the track' about 120 miles north of Alice.

Quite suddenly, a cloud of budgerigars crossed overhead, flying west to east. The migration continued for the next 50 miles, and after dark the Bartons could still hear the wings above them.

Budgerigars have been breeding in the N.T. for the past 10 months. The rains in Queensland must have triggered off the migration.[4]

Other similar observations have been made and have led to the belief by some that budgerigars actually migrate. However, migration infers a regular seasonal movement from one area to another. The movements of the budgerigars, on the other hand, are nomadic and have no set pattern although it appears that the birds have knowledge of the physical state of an area long before they arrive there. As naturalist, Vincent Serventy, notes, the budgerigars are not unlike other desert fauna in this respect,

Nomadism is common in desert animals and there may be a random scatter in search of food or water, or heading towards lightning flashes or rain clouds seen in the distance.

Still, there may be regular movement northwards in summer to meet the wet season and a return south to take advantage of winter rains.

Only continued research with banded birds will fill those gaps in our knowledge.[5]

So far, however, bird banding schemes to determine how budgerigars find their way have proved unrewarding and it is still not known if they are simply guided to new feeding grounds by instinct.[6]

Areas where budgerigars are located.

Arthur Menchin

Much of the following information on the budgerigar in the semi-arid (grazing and pastural) areas was gathered by amateur ornithologists (bushmen) like Arthur Menchin.

My interest in Arthur Menchin was stimulated by the reports of his vast knowledge of natural phenomena in general and birdlife in particular. Our first meeting occurred in Moree, New South Wales, in 1968, and since that time I have witnessed a form of charisma that he has in his relations with the birds and animals he handles. His first association with budgerigars was in the Mudgee district when, in 1920, at the age of ten, he stood in amazement at the sight of a huge assemblage of wild budgerigars. They had come in their millions and to his knowledge they have never again returned en masse into this district. The area, at the time, was used mainly for grazing and was lightly timbered, as such it provided an ideal place for budgerigars to breed in. In addition, there was an ample supply of seeding grass. Young Arthur, with the help of his sister, was able to catch a pair of budgerigars, which were nesting in a hollow limb. He kept the pair for pets, and since that time he has rarely been without these small parrots. Later in his life, living around the north west district of New South Wales he was to witness huge flocks coming and going many many times.

Moree is situated in the inland plains district which, with its black basalt soil, is very fertile and is generally associated with a good rainfall. These plains commence in the Wimmera area of Victoria and run almost continuously through New South Wales to the Gulf of Carpentaria in Queensland where they extend west into the Northern Territory and across to the Kimberleys in Western Australia. The rolling plains support creeks and tributaries, many of which feed permanent rivers. Some areas are devoid of timber and others support scattered trees that thicken in some areas to become heavily wooded. Tall tussock grasses often form a complete groundcover and the plains are the home of the native Mitchell grasses, the budgerigar's staple diet when they inhabit these regions.

After good spring or summer rains parts of this country look like huge wheat fields spreading endlessly on the horizon. A small portion, the Barkly Tablelands, which occupy 640 sq. km. (400 sq. miles) to the north west of Mt Isa (Qld) support the largest stand of Mitchell grass in Australia and budgerigars are seen there in countless numbers, as is borne out in the following field observation,

Budgerigar — Many flocks were seen in Southern Queensland, being numerous on the upper part of the Wilson River. They were not

seen when crossing the central drought area until near Headingly Station on the Georgina River, where several came to water. In the Gulf country they were in immense numbers. On our way down the Brook, on the Bourketown road, flocks of thousands were flushed from the ground almost continuously. The grass was two feet tall with seeding heads above it, and it produced an abundance of food, quite equal to the canary seed.

Across to the Leichhardt they were equally numerous and settled to feed in big flocks around our camp at the Leichhardt Falls. All the way up the Leichhardt in the open country they continued to rise in vast flocks and we flushed many from nesting hollows. These brilliant and beautiful little creatures seem in no danger of extermination. They feed on any kind of small grass or weed seeds, are always on the alert, are able to fly with the utmost rapidity.[7]

In 1966, when inland areas were in the grip of drought, budgerigars descended on the Moree district in the millions and, with an abundance of food in the area, breeding took place, after which the birds departed. They appeared again in 1972 but not in the numbers previously seen. Their first habit, on arrival, was to drink, and roll about in the wet couch grass growing at the edges of bore drains. However, as a result of saturating their feathers, many were then unable to fly, and were literally able to be picked up by the hundreds. The saline water in these drains is released at the piped bore head under pressure and is generally hot, although this quickly cools. I can recall one bore which releases 1½ million litres a day and another which supplies water to over 160 km (100 miles) of V-shaped drains. It was in these bore drains that the scenes of the disastrous bird holocaust were acted out in March 1932. A newspaper report at the time tells the story,

The hot blast has been disastrous to the birds in Western Queensland as well as the Northern Territory (*Bulletin*, 2-3-1932). In the Central West thousands fell dead amongst the trees, while many more sought refuge in houses. Many others perished in the bore drains, flying into water in which a human being could not bear to dip a hand. The effect of this paralysing dry heat has to be experienced to be understood.[8]

Arthur Menchin recalled that the flocks always arrived when the seeds of the native grasses were at the sappy stage, which meant that they were ripe when breeding was in progress. Their arrival in December 1972 he remembers well because it coincided with the harvesting of a paddock of Pannicum millet which, of course, the wild budgerigars relished.

In rare cases they have been known to attack ripening wheat crops but generally, they have a preference for small ripened seed — a fact proven both in the past and more recently by inspections of the crops of birds shot.

When feeding takes place the congregations of birds will sometimes number several thousand. They mainly feed in open grassland in early morning and late afternoon; at other times during the day smaller feeding flocks occur. These groups, consisting of males and females together, frequently change as congregations leave and others drop in.

Although the birds search for food independently of each other they always move in a cohesive unit in the one direction. Often drifting movements are performed as birds keep moving onto new ground, eating seeds from ground vegetation or those that have been dispersed through shedding. Other seeds are obtained from tall tussock grasses by climbing the tillers, or by alighting on the seedhead thus forcing the grass to the ground so that the seeds can be extracted.

Budgerigars, when seeking a place to nest show no preference for any particular species of tree, either dead or alive; their only requirement is that a suitably sized hole or concave can be found, preferably in the vicinity of surface water. They may also nest in logs on the ground, often with more than one pair to the log. Similarly, burrowing into the dirt to nest among the roots of fallen trees is not uncommon. A reference to some unusual nesting situations in the Lake Eyre Basin of South Australia was made in 1931,

Shell Parrots (*Melopsittacus undulatus*). These beautifully plumaged birds were in countless numbers along the Cooper and Diamantina, and were nesting almost everywhere. Whilst camped for lunch near Pandie Station, we were glad to make use of the shade provided by a fine spreading gum on the bank of the Diamantina, and during our stay we noted birds enter eight different hollows in this one tree, and though I did not investigate, I feel justified in saying each hollow contained a 'nest'. In this same gum was a Diamond Dove's nest and also a nest of the White-winged Caterpillar-eater. A little way along the river, I walked past a high creek bank, and was greatly surprised to see a Shell Parrot bustle out of a tunnelled hole in the bank. I at once investigated, and found that what was evidently a home of the Red-backed Kingfisher at one time recently had been used by the Shell Parrot as its cradle for its eggs. I enlarged the tunnel sufficiently to get an egg out, and was satisfied it belonged to Mrs Shelly. There were two more eggs in the hollow, so evidently the full clutch had yet to be completed.[9]

Budgerigars appear to breed in any but the winter months and as food abundance varies from place to place, so does the breeding cycle. Thus, at times, such as when there is an impending scarcity of food, the hen will lay only three eggs and in other instances, when the rainfall is meagre, a second brood may not occur.

Laying takes place on alternate days with average clutches of four to six white eggs. These usually rest in the earthy material which gathers in the rotting hollows of the tree. The hen incubates the eggs and nest inspection will reveal eggs or young or both in various stages of development.

In the early stages of hatching the cock feeds the hen at the entrance hole and she, in turn, feeds the young by the same process; regurgitation. Once all the eggs have hatched the nests are not difficult to locate because the young appear at the nest entrance on the return of their parents, both of which now share the feeding role. Their visits to the nest are at regular intervals, the period becoming longer as the youngsters grow older. At this stage it is not uncommon for a hen to lay a second brood even though the youngsters from the first may not yet have left the nest. Nevertheless, when the young leave the nest they are capable of looking after themselves although some will continue to beg for food.

During the budgerigars' visit to Moree in 1972 two clutches were produced over a five month period. Arthur Menchin watched these birds, after showers of rain, climb and flutter amongst the leaves of the trees, wetting themselves to bathe, and afterwards preening themselves while drying in the sunlight. On another occasion he noticed them flying in and out of a large, burnt-out hollow tree, and on closer inspection discovered the birds had been eating the charcoal on the inside of the trunk.

In the autumn the flocks began to show signs that they were preparing for departure. Arthur Menchin had observed this activity many times before. The budgerigars congregated in huge mobs and began to circle at a much greater height than they normally fly. They continued this activity at various intervals for about an hour, for two or three days. Arthur Menchin's theory is that they do this for exercise and to allow themselves to take their bearings on the direction they will take. On the day of departure the birds circle and fly off, unswerving unless scattered by predators.

On the day after departure an inspection of the scene revealed that some birds, apparently too old to make the journey, had remained behind. Also, many youngsters, at various stages of development had been left to die by their parents. These birds, some of which were only half-feathered, ventured from the nests in search of food, and soon fell easy prey to crows, butcher birds and many other predators.

Predators

Budgerigars have very few predators to contend with and their principal enemies are falcons. Although most kills are made only when budgerigars are in full flight, there is immediate silence when the whistling sound of the Black Falcon is heard by the birds in the trees. Birds that are feeding on the plains either dart for cover into nearby scrub or lose their heads completely and fly straight into open country where they soon fall prey to the bold antagonist.

It is doubtful that predators have a huge effect on budgerigar numbers and it would appear that the most cruel effect on budgerigar numbers is wrought by natural occurrences, such as heat-waves and drought, hail storms and bush fires. The effect of heat-waves, in particular, has been well recorded. For example, during the great bird holocaust of 1932. At this time, temperatures in some areas reached 124°F in the shade and at Oodnadatta in South Australia the average shade temperature for fifty-one days from December was 110°F.[10] The effects of the intense heat was disastrous for the budgerigars and they died in tens of thousands. In desperation they sought shelter from the searing heat of the sun around houses and railway sidings[11] and many a birdlover put out water receptacles and filled troughs for the birds. In some areas, however, the farmers were driven to cover wells and tanks* containing their valuable water supply because these were being rapidly inundated by the

Typical feeding grounds for budgerigars in Western Australia is this spinifex country. The spinifex grass seeds often provide a year round source of food.

Dungalear Artesian Bore in New South Wales which began flowing at the rate of 90,920 gallons per day on the 23rd of February 1924.

birds and their pumps were being choked by their corpses.[12] Some estimated that the numbers of budgerigars to die at the time were in the millions.

At Kokatha Station, situated between Lakes Harris, Everard and Gairdner, and about 30 miles south-west of Kingoonya Station on the Trans-Australian railway line, Mr Reg. Wilson stated that 'the Shell Parrots (*Melopsittacus undulatus*) must have died in millions'. From one of his dams he said he took out and burnt five tons of Parrots. 'We made a net with wire-netting' he said 'and dragged it from one side to the other and then extracted the birds, as the fisherman does his fish. We filled a petrol tin and weighed it, and then by counting the tins were able to arrive at the weight. From one of the tanks we took 30,000 dead Parrots. The birds would settle on the water for a drink; others would follow and push them under the water; and this went on until dead bodies were many inches thick.[13]

In 1973-74 parts of the Nullarbor Plain in Western Australia had approximately four times its normal rainfall. This produced an abundance of plant growth so that the budgerigars bred freely in this area. In late 1974 bushfires swept through the area stripping the land so that the budgerigar's food

supply was destroyed. The results, as reported in the press at the time, were tragic,

Perth — An appeal to help save the Nullarbor's dying budgerigars was made yesterday by a councillor from a Perth suburb. Mrs Jean Goadby, of Nedlands, appealed to travellers to take packets of bird seed to scatter on the road across the Nullarbor. Mrs R. Rintel, who recently crossed the Plain, said she and her husband had seen thousands of budgerigars dead on the road, either overcome by bushfire smoke or hit by motorists. But the director of South Perth Zoo, Dr Tom Spence, said any birdseed lift might be in vain. Nature would take its course following two good budgie breeding seasons in succession. He said: 'Australia is a savage country. What will happen is that the budgerigars will be decimated anyway'.[14]

Nevertheless, with all these calamities the budgerigar still survives and a good season will result in the numbers being quickly built up again.

Footnote:
*Tanks — Large man made reservoirs. They are excavated in the ground and have sloping banks which are generally 4.9 m (16 ft) deep. Their approximate capacity is nine thousand cubic metres (two million gallons) of water.

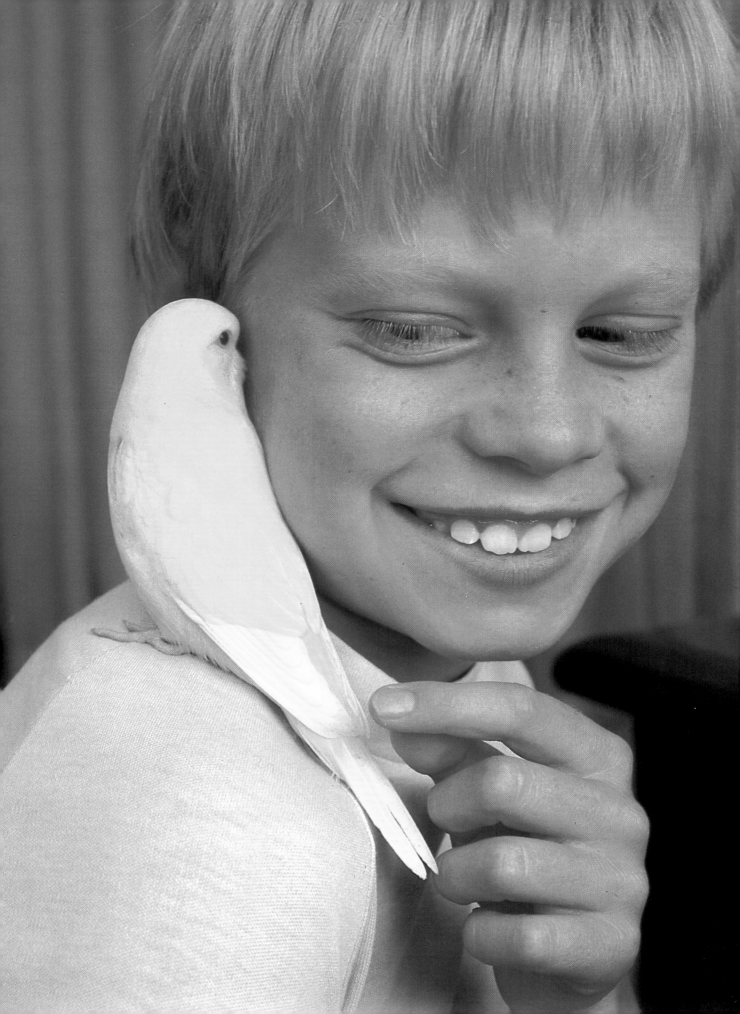

3 THE BUDGERIGAR AS A PET

No book on budgerigars would be complete without reference being made to the budgerigar's wonderful adaptability in becoming the most widely loved of all pets. For every exhibition breeder there are thousands of owners of pets in a cage. In addition their familiar chirp is heard, albeit in a foreign language, all over the world, and yes, the ancestors of these budgerigars also originated in Australia.

The pet industry has been responsible for the spread of these native Australians to overseas countries. In America today the immense pet market is a highly respected business. The main source of supply of parakeets (budgerigars) is from the large number of bird-breeding farms widespread throughout the United States. This industry commenced in Europe in the nineteenth century and developed into a large-scale business: one establishment in Toulouse was reputed in the late 1880s to have had in the vicinity of fifteen thousand budgerigars. The first mention of a budgerigar talking was published in France in 1847, although it was a record of an event that actually took place in Sydney. The first talking budgerigar recorded in Europe spoke German and Dr Karl Russ states in his book, *The Speaking Parrots* (1884), that Miss E. Maier of Stuttgart was, in 1877, the first to give an account of a talker in this species. Her young grass parakeet (budgerigar), which had not yet attained its adult plumage, picked up some lovely notes from the song of a Japanese robin.

It was very tame, and at a call would fly to my shoulder or my hand. Then it learnt the trumpet notes of a pair of zebra finches and forgot the call of the robin. I therefore sent the finches away so that 'Misse' — as I had named the parakeet — had no intercourse with other birds and soon it also forgot the robin trumpeting. How great was my astonishment and delight when one day it greeted me with the words 'Come dear little misse come' which it at first pronounced hesitatingly, but soon loudly and distinctly. I had always saluted it thus in the mornings, but without the intention of teaching it to speak. Not long afterwards it began to say also 'Oh you dear little misse, you little darling, come and give me a kiss'. It is most charming to see it and hear it, when it plays with my finger, kissing it, then singing and trying to eat it. It flys away, returns and repeats these gambols countless times, during which it continually chatters the above words.[1]

Dr Russ also states that Mr W. Bauer of Tübingen sent one of these parakeets (budgerigars) to a show for talking parrots in Berlin and was awarded a medal. He afterwards sold the bird for £7 10s.

The English naturalist, Gould, in his book *Handbook to the Birds of Australia, vol 2* wrote;

As cage birds they are as interesting as can possibly be imagined, for independently of their highly ornamental appearance they are constantly coquetting, squabbling and assuming every variety of graceful position. Their inward song which cannot well be described is unceasingly warbled forth from morn till night and is even continued throughout the night if they are placed in a room where an animated conversation is carried on.[2]

From this description, it seems quite appropriate that the early settlers should have given budgerigars names like 'the warbling parrot' and 'the canary parrot'.

It was not unusual for the early Australian settlers to be confronted with a homeless young parrot that was unable to fend for itself. These farmers quite often returned home at night with a young parrot tucked down the front of their shirts or in a coat pocket. I doubt if many of these parrots were ever kept for long periods because of the unavailability of seed suitable for them. Oats was the only seed that was suitable; wheat and corn had to be cracked or soaked before they could be given to the birds. Seedling native grasses could have been used also but would have been unavailable in many periods.

Children and budgerigars go well together. This six week old cock bird has already found a firm friend.

I have observed that there are three instances when youngsters of all parrot life in the wild may find themselves homeless. The first is when trees are chopped down to make way for new pastures or for material use. Then one often finds that after the tree has hit the ground the youngsters emerge unhurt from splintered limbs.

The second instance occurs when the youngsters are nearing the fully feathered stage. At this time they frequent the nest-entrance hole and because some of these holes look down to the ground the young birds lose their grip and fall out. Other entrance holes may have a branch or limb adjacent to them which the birds will walk along for exercise, lose their grip through over-confidence and, with a feeble flutter, find themselves on the ground. The bird is then unable to return to the nest and it is in vain that parrots will congregate around the youngsters trying to coax them to rise in the air and fly back to the safety of the nest.

A third cause of homelessness is when the feed in an area is running low and the nomadic urge commences. The flock contains many parent birds with young still in the nest in all stages of development, and these parent birds leave the area regardless of their waiting brood. The young are left to starve to death. Hunger may cause the largest of the young to venture from the nest and they can be seen running around on the ground, unable to fly off in search of food.

I have known bushmen to pick up parrots at these times and to begin feeding them until they were old enough to crack seed and feed themselves. Feeding them at the early stage is achieved by numerous, and often unusual, methods. The feed used is mainly breakfast cereals, especially rolled oats, which is prepared in a soft state. I remember a chap who used to feed these birds by putting a little on his bottom lip and drawing the youngster on his hand close to his mouth. The hungry bird would soon take his first taste of food from his pouted lips and then continue feeding. The budgerigar was totally reared in this manner.

These wild budgerigars became very tame and before they were able to fly one wing was clipped to restrict their flight. The birds then had the run of the house or hut and were only put into a makeshift cage when no one was in attendance, and at night. People may not realise that a lot of parrots, especially cockatoos and galahs, are taken from their nests in the wild each year. Some of these become very tame and are excellent tricksters and talkers: the same is possible with a wild budgie.

Regular feeding of tidbits is the first step in training.

Budgerigars, especially males, make excellent household pets. Because of their small size they do not have the destructive and damaging effects on household property that most members of the parrot family have. Also, unlike the canary who will not whistle when moulting, the budgerigar will talk throughout the year. Because they take up very little room and the cost of feeding is relatively cheap, they make an ideal companion for elderly folk or a person living alone. When owned by a family they seem to become more attached to a child. In all cases their biggest asset is their ability to talk; they are excellent mimics and few sounds escape them.

Cages

Before you purchase your pet, your first concern should be a cage to accommodate it. If more than one bird is kept then the cage should of course be larger. An ideal cage would be at least 600 mm (2 ft) in length. The height and width no less than 300 mm (1 ft) with bars spaced no more than 12 mm (½ in) apart. These bars are better for the bird to climb if they are running horizontal rather than vertical. It is important that the length be adequate for the birds to be able to exercise: I have known birds in small areas to become more like humming birds. They seem to develop the ability to exercise their wings as in flight while remaining stationary in mid-air.

Cages are generally made of metal although there are some fold-up varieties which are made from bamboo and wood. Although the latter are very ornamental they are unsuitable for budgerigars because they will be chewed by the budgie and gaping holes will appear. A galvanised or chrome cage is the most serviceable and will last many years. If you are buying a painted one make sure it is baked enamel as ordinary paint will soon be chewed off. A nice cage stand or a simple hook may be needed for the positioning of the cage.

The door of the cage is very important and should be spring-loaded. If not, you will have to keep it closed with a clothes peg to ensure the bird does not open it with its beak. A removable slide tray in the cage bottom is ideal for easy cleaning. Check to see if it is equipped with a carrying handle, which is also useful for hanging the cage. Check your cage before buying it to see there are no projecting wire ends that can catch a bird's wing or the ring it may be wearing on its leg.

Cats and birds can get along together, but only under strict supervision.

Some cages are equipped with plastic bottoms and sides that extend 75 mm (3 in) up the bars. If yours does not have this feature there are plastic strips which can be purchased to do the same job. This prevents the seed husks and feathers from being strewn over the surrounding area. Before you use the cage, wash it with detergent and hot water to remove any harmful acids.

Perches

Perches should not be overlooked and must be of wood so the claws are able to grip them. There should be at least two: these can vary in shape and size but the diameters should be no less than 10 mm (⅜ in) wide. They should be roughened up and cleaned regularly with sand paper or steel wool. Budgerigars also love swings and one swing hanging from the top of the cage is ideal. Perches and swings enable the birds to exercise feet and claws.

cage birds and should be scattered on the floor of the cage or placed in containers. Grit is essential in the diet of the budgerigar because it helps them to grind food internally. A piece of cuttle-fish bone, clipped to the inside of the cage helps in food-grinding and is also a source of calcium.

Greens

These are fed regularly, mainly in the morning. If your bird appears to have diarrhoea and looks loose and stained around the vent stop supplying green feed until all these signs have disappeared. A comprehensive guide to the feeding of seeds and greenfoods is provided in the chapter on Feeding.

Selecting your bird

The purchase of your bird or birds may not be easy, particularly if you are looking for some rarer colour combinations. Remember, colour does not affect a bird's talking ability so if you simply require a talker, colour will not affect your choice. On the other hand you should choose a bird whose appearance and colour appeals to you as you will have to become fond of it if you are going to train it successfully.

It is a general rule that cocks or males make the best talkers. Some hens may talk but it will take a lot of patience to teach them. Cocks tame easily and generally have a gentler nature. Hens are more nervous and will bite when being spiteful; they are much harder to tame. I have heard of a male budgerigar beginning to talk at the age of eighteen months, however most will have commenced to talk before they are six months old.

What age?

The bird should be purchased as soon as it leaves the nest and is capable of cracking seed and feeding itself. It is then six to seven weeks old and still very quiet and easy to tame. Budgies at this stage of life are called *barred heads* or *unbroken caps*.

A youngster's age is reasonably easy to determine. The feathering is somewhat softer in colour than an adult's and most varieties of birds have barrings (zebra markings), see page 107 for identification drawing, which commence just above the cere or nostril and extend over the back of the head. After their first moult, (in most varieties) at about three months of age, the budgerigars get their adult plumage and lose the barrings on the front of their head. Also, after the first moult the mask colour or bib colour (that is, in the area under

Toys

As with children's toys there seems to be no end to the quantity and quality of toys for birds. However, you should not confuse your budgerigar by cluttering up the cage. Instead, substitute the toys periodically and this will enable you to discover the pet's likes and dislikes, particularly when a new toy is given.

There are many kinds of see-saws, ladders, toy birds and roly-polys, as well as various bells which they love to ring. When allowed to perform outside the cage they can be given toys on a string which they can take in their beak and pull along. Nevertheless, a mirror is possibly the best purchase because it enables the budgerigar to think he has a companion. As birds seem to spend a lot of time in front of the mirror it should be placed so that the bird can stand on its perch and see clearly the reflection of its head. The bird will chatter away in front of the mirror, sometimes regurgitating food to the image. This behaviour is perfectly normal and reveals that the bird is in good health.
Bird baths that clip on to the lift-up door are available and these are ideal. You will find that the birds become accustomed to their regular bath, especially when they are moulting. A few drops of glycerine added periodically to their bath will help to put a sheen on their feathers.

Grit

Many different varieties of grit are available. These contain minerals and salts especially prepared for

By sitting calmly rather than flying away, this baby shows ideal temperament for a pet.

A healthy six week old cock bird.

31

their bottom beak), extends to a point on the skull just past the eye and the mask (bib) area which contained lots of flecking should be replaced by six well-defined spots, when they get their adult plumage.

A fourth indication of age is the eye. The white iris ring does not fully appear in a budgerigar's eye until about six months after they are born. Up until then the iris is black. The beaks may also be black at an early age although they vary in colour according to the variety of bird.

Never be talked into buying a baby with a bright blue or nut-brown cere as they are too old.

Sexing

Determining the sex of a bird is much more difficult than determining its age. Even experts are not always accurate at sexing a lot of birds at this baby stage. However, here are some general guidelines: the cere of the cock is rather plump and pale blue in colour while a hen's cere is flatter and paler and generally tinged white around the nostrils. If you are seeking a yellow or white bird the task of sexing is a lot harder.

Covering cages

If a bird is to be kept in a room that is lighted for long periods at night, a covering may be needed so that it can get some sleep and rest. Remember that birds commence their day at first light if it is visible to them. The covering for the cage can be made of any material so long as it reduces the light, although plastic covers are available on the market. The cage can be covered partially or fully depending on the climate, but make sure the bird is not in any draughts. If you have cats in the house it is advisable to cover the bird fully at night and at any time when unattended.

Feeding utensils

Various kinds of feeders are available, but the one with the largest outlet is preferable, especially in the tube feeders. Open dishes and clip on seed pots can be purchased in plastic or glass but metal pots, if available, are ideal because they are strongest.

Feeding

A budgerigar will not survive after twenty-four hours without seed and it is of the utmost importance that you ensure your bird always has seed. When you leave your bird in another person's care, you should for their sake inform them of the bird's need for seed. If you purchase a mixed seed take care when opening it, that it does not smell musty. Then, if using self-feeders, make sure all the types of seed run freely out of the bottom outlet and do not clog. This problem may occur with the cylindrical self-feeder, many of which are made for water use.

Another problem with seed is caused by a fodder moth. In the hatching stage one cocoon will sometimes attach itself to the inside of the outlet. This causes others to accumulate in the same area and gradually the flow of seed is reduced. Eventually, if not removed, they will block the passage completely. The same problem will occur if water has been spilt or spurted on the container and allowed to run into the seed. It is a good idea to clean the outlet with your finger every few days.

Open seed vessels must continually have the husks blown from the top of the seed. It may appear at times that the bowl is half full of seed but after the husk is removed you will be surprised to see just how little actual seed is left.

Water utensils

There are various tube and clip-on drinkers as well as open vessels of all shapes and sizes. I prefer an open glass dish or glazed vessel that has a rounded bottom and no corners. These may be more prone to breakages but they have no corners to try and clean and are therefore much more hygienic.

Water and bathing

Many drinkers, if used continuously, will acquire an unpleasant odour and green algae will appear. They must be thoroughly washed and cleaned in a salt solution or one of the bottle-wash solutions available for infants' bottles. Your main concern is to keep all vessels clean and free from droppings that may contaminate the water.

Often birds that are let out in the house like to drink from a dripping tap. They will also bathe under it if the water drips on to an upturned bowl.

Rung birds

In countries south of the equator breeding seasons for the budgerigar breeders generally begin on 1 June each year and last till the end of May in the following year. At the beginning of each breeding season budgerigar clubs issue rings dated for that year. These birds are referred to as *club rung birds*. Do not be confused if you are purchasing a baby in February and you find that it has the number of the previous year on it.

In countries north of the equator ring issues date from 1 January and the breeding season covers the full calendar year.

Novelty birds

I would not buy birds called *mops* or *feather dusters*. These are large birds with long twisted feathers. Rarely are they able to stand on a perch or fly. They do not chirp but squawk and they eat endlessly although their life span is very short: the longest lived I have heard of was nine months.

I also do not recommend the buying of *runners* or *hikers*. These birds lose all their flight and tail feathers, and in extreme cases their body feathers. This condition, called *French Moult*, has been with us since the 1880s. Much research has been carried out but no positive cause or cure has been ascertained. In some cases the feathers may grow again but this cannot be guaranteed. More informa-tion on this condition is provided in the chapter, Diseases and Ailments.

Taming

The best method to tame any bird is to place green-food or tidbits between the bars of the cage. While the bird is eating, slowly place your hand quite near. Repeat, and after a few days the bird will let you scratch its neck with your finger. After the bird has become quite used to this you can start to train it to perch on a stick. (*Note*: all movements must be carried out slowly and quietly so as not to frighten the bird.) A small perch or a stick can be manoeuvred into the cage and, if gently pressed across the front of its legs, will cause the bird to become unbalanced and step on to the stick. You can then lift the bird up and down on it. After some

Constant attention strengthens the bond between the bird and members of the family.

time you will be able to finger-tame the bird in this same manner inside the cage.

As birds seem to be more quiet and placid after dark you may get better results at night. After the bird has become finger-tame you can slowly take it out of the cage, for a short time at first. Then lengthen the time gradually until the bird becomes accustomed to its new surroundings. The budgie may fly off, so make sure all the windows and doors, if not fitted with insect screens, are closed.

Remain still and the bird may return to you. If not, move quietly towards it, uttering a familiar sound to restore the bird's confidence in you. You may put your finger out for the bird to climb on to and then return it to the cage. Soon the bird will eagerly await this freedom, especially if it becomes a regular daily occurrence.

The most widely used method of cutting wings is set out in eight simple steps below. Remember, the scissors used in this or any other method must be absolutely sharp.

Cutting the wings

If a bird is hard to tame and train, or you wish to restrict its movements, you may do what some pet trainers do, that is, cut the wing feathers.

One method is to cut only one wing which in some cases means the bird is unable to fly because of the unevenness of the wings. The correct feathers to cut are the seven to nine flight feathers which are the longest and last feathers on the wing.

Another method is to cut a few feathers on both wings leaving the last three feathers. This process of cutting the wings evenly is more attractive and allows the bird to still fly although it cannot go too far. The cutting of the wing feathers will not hurt the bird but care should be taken not to cut them too far down the quill because this may result in bruising and bleeding at the feather base.

The wing feathers, after being cut, will not

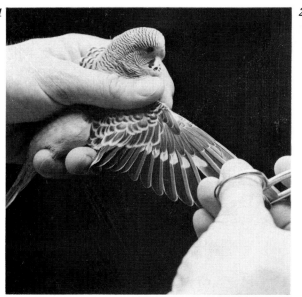

1

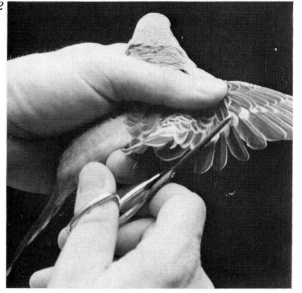

2

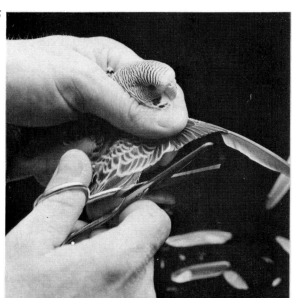

5

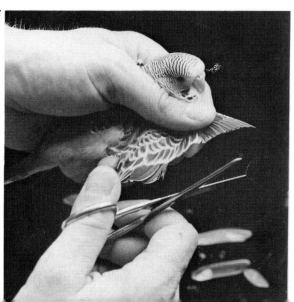

6

regrow until the bird has moulted or the stumps are removed by pulling them out in a direct line with the feather growth.

Training to talk

When training your budgerigar to talk it is important that it is not able to hear any other bird. A good teacher is generally one whose voice tends to be soft. At first, it is a good idea to cover half the cage so you can get the bird's whole attention. Also, have the cage at eye level. Begin teaching by repeating the same word, such as 'Hello' or the bird's name. Soon you will notice your bird sitting with his head cocked to one side, listening intently. A few words, spoken often by the same person, will give the best results. It may take from three to six months for the bird to say its first word. After it has learnt to talk, introduce other words, one at a time. When one sentence has been learnt, introduce another. The bird will soon be picking up sentences and words it should not repeat.

The budgerigar can also be taught to whistle. A few opening bars is best at first and in no time your bird will be whistling a tune. Soon you will be amazed at the sounds your bird will learn to mimic without being taught. Some people even use tape recorders to record and teach birds to talk.

House rules

The general rule is to take care, very great care. You must always be on the alert when your pet is out of its cage, especially if it is wearing a leg ring which can easily become entangled on the simplest of objects. One of the worst hazards for flying pets are fires, especially at night. I have observed that towards sundown budgerigars seem to lose a lot of their vision. They will fly into an open fire, or radiator, especially if the room is in darkness. On

the other hand take care that windows have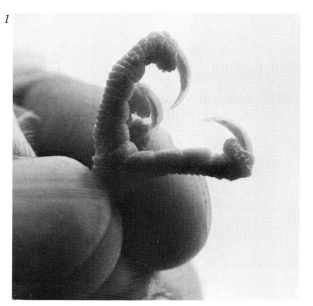
curtains across them to protect the bird from flying
straight into them. This can also happen with large
mirrors. After flying directly into these a bird can
become concussed and may die several days later.
Other potential causes of fatality are basins, sinks
and baths containing water, and draughts. Never
leave your pet budgerigar in a draught as this will
quickly cause a fatal illness. On the other hand, in
extremely hot weather, make sure the bird is
comfortable by placing a damp towel partially over
the cage. This is also a good plan when travelling by
car in the hot weather.

When placing your bird outside make sure it has
partial shade. If a budgerigar is left in direct or even
reflected sunlight on very hot days blindness and
even death can be the result in a very short space
of time. Another good point when you are placing
the cage outside is to make sure it is protected
from domestic pets and wild birds: butcher birds,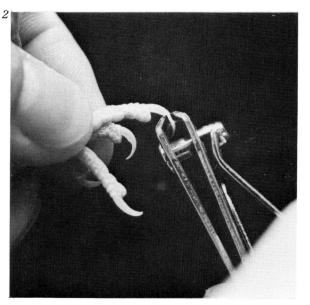
currawongs and magpies love to molest caged birds
and they often cause the bird's death.

Health care

You may at times have to trim your pet's claws and
beak. When we trim our nails there is no pain and
the bird does not suffer either. Cage birds can
develop long nails that may curve backwards,
making it impossible for the bird to grip the perch.
These can be trimmed with nail clippers. Before
you start note where the vein ends in the nail and
be sure not to cut into this. When you cut the nail
always make the cut on an inward angle so that a
point is left on the nail for gripping the perch.

Similarly, with an overgrown beak — observe
where the vein ends. Because the beak is normally
shaped to a near point, I find concave clippers ideal.
The best method is to cut the point first to the
desired length, then trim the sides. You can smooth
it off with a nail file or emery board. The same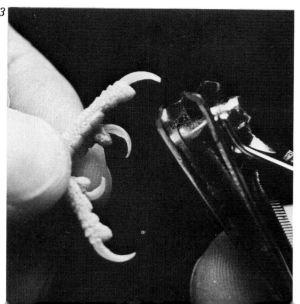
procedure is followed for the bottom beak. When
finished check to see that the beak closes correctly.

A cock's cere may turn brown giving an outward
appearance of being a hen. This is a hormone
break-down which generally occurs later in their
life, but is not a cause for alarm because it has no
effect on the bird's well-being.

Egg laying

Many people become distressed when a hen caged

*Three steps to safe claw trimming. It's safer to cut a little
at a time.*

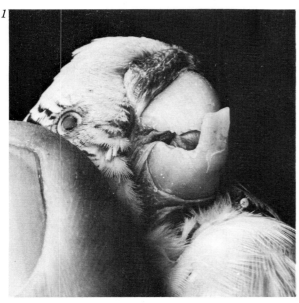

on her own begins to lay eggs. She may even begin to sit on them in one corner of the cage. Unless the hen has been mated to a cock the eggs will not be fertile and therefore will not hatch. This is a perfectly normal cycle and does no harm to the bird unless she becomes egg-bound. This condition is explained in the chapter, Diseases and Ailments. Early removal of the egg may help to stop the hen from laying any more eggs.

All in all budgies are generally hardy little birds and if the few basic rules for pet care are followed, your pet will reward you with many years of enjoyment and happiness.

Three steps to trimming an undershot beak. Check the position of the clippers before cutting. (See also page 51.)

The correct way to hold a budgerigar firmly but not tightly. In this position the bird cannot injure itself or bite you.

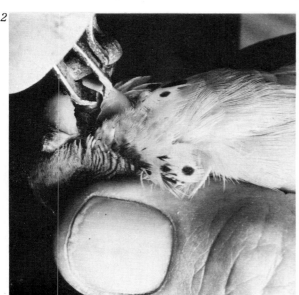

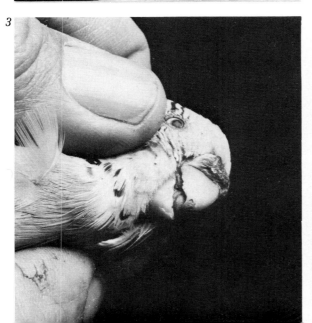

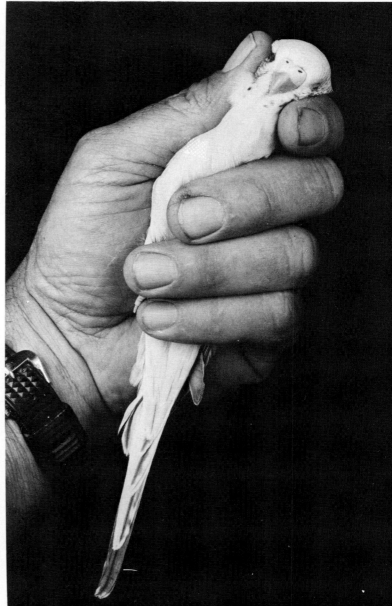

4 FEEDING

The budgerigar will survive on just seed and water but the four most important items for a healthy diet are seed, grit, calcium and water. It must be remembered that birds in their wild state utilise a much wider variety of foods and minerals. These have been available to budgerigars from the time of their evolution and I believe that the more natural the resources we supply, the better results we will have. I will give a broad description of the feeds available. This will enable you to work out your own feeding pattern to produce the best results. The main object is to have your birds healthy and vigorous at all times.

A balanced ration to fulfil their bodily requirements in the correct proportions would include proteins, carbohydrates, fats, minerals and salts. All these are contained in varying quantities in seeds and greenfoods. Vitamins, which have become an everyday topic for us all, are very complex. The five vitamin groups mainly concerning budgerigars are:

Vitamin A Necessary for young birds and the health of the skin and feathers.

Vitamin B The main source of physical energy, and essential for the smooth running of the nervous system.

Vitamin C Deficiency causes skin diseases.

Vitamin D Its presence is vital in the formation of bone, its absence causes rickets.

Vitamin E Prevents sterility and increases fertility.

It is possible to give overdoses of vitamins so care should be taken if these are being administered. Some of the problems associated with vitamin supplements will be dealt with in the chapter on Diseases and Ailments.

There is only one golden rule, check your seed hoppers and pots to make sure the birds have their daily requirements and make doubly sure you are not just looking at seed husks. The birds will die in twenty-four hours if no seed is available to them.

Feed time with greens on the floor of the aviary. A balanced diet is the single most important factor in the bird's life.

Seeds

The subject of seeds and their food value is by far the most important for caged birds. This is overlooked by many although there is much scientific data available on it. Let us start with the soil, which most people would think has very little

A commercial budgerigar seed mixture.

Millet sprays, left to right, White, Japanese, Pannicum.

bearing on this subject. All plant life is dependent on a large number of trace elements that are mostly found in the soil. This chemical process, taking place between soil and plant, is very complex. The end result is consumed by our birds and for this reason we should give more thought to this relationship.

If plant life lacks certain trace elements it shows in its growth, other deficiencies are only apparent with the testing of the seed. Insecticides also raise problems, as many have found with fatal results to their birds. When crops are sprayed in paddocks adjoining seed paddocks, the wind drift can carry the insecticide for miles, contaminating everything in its path. Tests with hawks have been carried out and the hawks have been found to contain amounts of D.D.T.: seed-eating parrots are their main source of food in the wild. If insecticide sprays have been used in our own garden greenfoods should be avoided and a mixed seed diet preferred. This will allow your birds to consume the trace and vitamin elements required without the risk of an insecticide intake.

No analysis will show us the most important characteristic of foodstuffs, that is, palatability. This can only be achieved by observation and we find that budgerigars, like humans, have likes and dislikes. Some birds have a strong liking for certain types of seeds and others will barely touch them even though they may contain a higher nutritive value. The staple diet in the past was a large proportion of pannicum millet, with a small amount of canary seed added. One rarely sees good pannicum now, so like the English fanciers I feed a greater proportion of canary seed. I must stress at this point that you should be wary of large canary seed as I have heard reports of it swelling in the crop, piercing the lining and causing the birds to haemorrhage and die. Apparently this was more evident in young birds being fed by their parents.

Japanese millet is a very good seed especially when the birds are breeding. It is much easier to husk because it is a softer type of seed. There are two varieties of Japanese millet, one is a nice brown colour, which I find the birds prefer, and the other is a grey colour and has a furry husk. White pearl millet is a little large for my liking but I have noticed that the plate millet, which is a little smaller, is used extensively in the United Kingdom. If red millet is available young birds seem to relish it. A small percentage of linseed in your mixture is beneficial because of its oil content. Small striped sunflower seeds may be placed in pots on its own but the

quantity should be limited for it tends to make the birds fat. Oats, whole or hulled, are always consumed readily and are most beneficial in cold weather as they tend to warm the blood. Oats should also be fed in individual pots.

Rape and niger seed are useful but the prices are prohibitive. A mixture of equal parts of various millets and the canary seed would be ideal, although I am not suggesting you try to incorporate all varieties at once. Most produce stores supply a varied seed mixture in either bulk or in packets. If the birds are picking over the seed and leaving a particular type, mix a smaller amount of this type in next time: it will be a trial and error task till you learn the birds' preferences. The only additive to mix with dry seed in my opinion is cod liver oil, which is beneficial prior to the breeding season to help the laying process. This can be mixed in thoroughly in the proportion of one teaspoon to 500 ml (1 pt) of seed and left overnight. Then mix the oily seed in equal parts with ordinary seed so that the birds can eat some with oil and some without. The same ratio of oil to seed can also be mixed with hulled oats, which absorb it better. Only one week's supply of seed should be mixed at one time because the oil may become rancid.

Care must be taken with storage of seed. If storing in bags, the area must be mouseproofed. If storing in clean drums or containers keep these off the floor or on a platform to avoid dampness. The safest way to prevent weevil and moth infestation, is to place a teaspoon of oil of eucalyptus on a piece of felt and put it on top of the seed and seal the container. Before you plan to use any seed stored this way take the lid off and leave for a few days, and then make sure it has not turned sour because we have no idea how old the seed is when we purchase it.

If one is uncertain of the quality of the seed a simple test is easily performed by placing 100 seeds between two sheets of blotting paper or cloth. Keep damp for a few days and count the ungerminated seeds, subtract this number from 100 and the remainder will give you the germination rate within a range of 10%. Standard germination test on canary seed is around 65%, millets are around 75%. This germination rate is important because a seed without its reproductive germ is dead and nearly useless as a food source. Seed for sowing is often government-certified using a germination test and if it does not reach the required percentage it will not be approved: these failed seeds are either dumped or sold as stock or poultry feeds. Never purchase seed that smells musty or has lumps of seed clinging together; it may have been harvested damp or have become wet in transit or storage. Its use will prove fatal to the budgerigar because it is certain to have fungus disease. A simple way to estimate the quality of the seed you are buying is to wet a finger, place it in the seed and examine it with the palm side up. Another pointer when buying in bag lots is the weight; better quality seed is much heavier. For instance, premium grade wheat can weigh up to 6 kg a bushel more than fair average quality wheat with the same moisture content.

Unfortunately for cage birds, very little work has been carried out on the composition and digestibility of the foodstuffs available. The only useful information available is a result of research in the poultry industry.

Soaked seed

Soaked or sprouted seed appears to be very beneficial to budgerigars, particularly during the breeding season. The only other times that this feeding is advantageous is when extra nourishment is required after some sickness, or when youngsters have just left the nest. Its use should be restricted to these instances, however, because when adult birds are not breeding they become too fat and docile on this diet.

Germination of grain placed in water or in contact with moisture commences within one hour. In the chemical process that follows starch is dissolved into dextrine which is easily digestible and quickly assimilated by the bloodstream. This eliminates a

Popular types of seeds: clockwise they are Japanese Millet, Red Millet, Canary, White Millet, Pannicum Millet. Centre, Hulled Oats.

lot of stress for the parent birds during feeding and in return the youngsters respond rapidly with plump growth and fluffy down.

The best seed for soaking is wheat or, full or hulled oats, although I find hulled oats tend to break up. For daily use, place the seed in a bucket and cover with water, soak for about twenty-four hours: harder wheats can take up to forty-eight hours for the skin to become soft enough. Rinse the seed till the water becomes clear and drain — it is ready to use. If you give your birds any additive like powdered yeast or beef extract, this can now be added to the soaked seed. A stainless steel cooking oil filter is also very useful for soaking seed, especially if it fits neatly onto a 10 L (2 gal) plastic bucket filled with water, because it can be easily removed for rinsing under the tap. If you do not wish to provide soaked seed, you may give the birds brown bread soaked in milk instead, or powdered products such as Complan. These are given by many breeders in the United Kingdom.

Any seed can also be mixed and sprouted. A simple method for sprouting is to place the seed between two moist jute sacks. Mechanical sprouters are available too — they are used for sprouting grains used in vegetarian diets and Asian style cooking.

Greens

The benefits of greenfood and seeding grasses to birds are much under-rated by the average bird keeper. Their use is important because they contain oil, vitamins and mineral trace elements, some of which are lost in the process of ripening and drying. Some European fanciers deep freeze greenfood for use during the harsh winters.

In most countries, a supply of seedling grasses, herbs and cultivated species is available at all times. These could include wild millets, wild oats, summer and winter grasses and cultivated silver beet and Chinese spinach. A good guide, if you are unsure of a particular seed grass, is to watch wild birds — if they eat it you can be assured it is all right. Probably the most poisonous weed is the petty's purge or milk weed. It can be found in gardens and has green almost circular leaves and minute yellow flowers. When its stem is broken sharply a milky juice is exuded which is a strong caustic poison, an old cure for warts.

Paspalum is also harmful, especially if it is near the ripening stage when a gluey substance forms around the seed. Children quite often break out in sores after playing in it at this stage.

Poisonous milkweed and its dangerous sap.

Poisonous milkweed.

When seed grasses are given, the budgerigars will always prefer the grasses with smaller seeds. Perhaps this is because they are more nutritious. Mouses ear (chick weed) is the best green available because it contains a small seed and the birds relish the leaves and the stalks. It is also rich in vitamin E which helps fertility. Common dandelion, not the English type, is also an excellent green in early winter and the birds extract the juices from its stems. Similarly with silver beet. I like to pick this very early in the morning while the dew is still on it because the budgerigars seem to like the extra

One type of wild oat

Shepherds Purse

One type of wintergrass

Chickweed, or mouse's ear.

moisture, however, it is not advisable to give birds greenfoods that have unmelted frost on them because this can result in enteritis. Carrots and apples cut in halves are eaten and many berries from ornamental trees and vines are also beneficial. Budgerigars will likewise devour sweet corn when it is in its milky stage on the cob.

The best time to feed greens is in the early mornings, some seem to have a purging effect if given later in the day. Shepherds purse, on the other hand, is of a hot nature, and its nutritious properties act as a stimulant to the stomach,

thereby reducing the scours. Hanging wire baskets or a looped chain can be used to hold your seedling grasses in the aviaries. Stale grasses must be removed daily before they can ferment and become poisonous. Another idea is to place potted grasses and greenfoods in your aviaries. These can be removed from time to time to enable them to recuperate for further use.

Branches of most trees are readily stripped and gnawed at by budgerigars extracting the cellulose from the bark, but here again be wary of some poisonous ornamental types. Eucalyptus are preferred, especially the leaves and the seed pods. Have the branches hanging downwards so that the birds can avoid getting their rings caught on the small twigs, and place them where birds are unlikely to crash into them when they are disturbed unexpectedly.

To keep greens for up to a week place in a plastic bag in your refrigerator. An alternative method is to place them in a bucket of water like a bunch of flowers.

By osmosis greens such as silver beet can be used to introduce some minerals and salts to the diet. Salt, for instance, can be mixed with water, and when the stalks of the silver beet are placed in the liquid the salts are absorbed into the plant membrane. If, however, the silver beet leaves have turned yellow the next day, your salt content is too great and needs to be reduced.

Soils

If your birds cannot go to the soil, bring the soil to them. The soil structure and its contents vary greatly from area to area and your budgerigars will benefit if you are able to give them soil from a wide range of places. Sods or grasses with soil around their roots are relished by birds. This soil teems with invisible life — bacteria, fungi and insects. Also present are minerals, trace elements, and roughage. As with greenfoods make sure the grasses have not been fouled by animals or sprayed with insecticides and that snail baits have not been recently laid in the soil.

If earth floors are used in aviaries they should be forked over regularly. A little lime and dolomite could be spread over before digging to stop the soil from becoming sour. There is only one method of sterilising this soil correctly and this involves using methyl bromine which is a deadly poison; I would not recommend it. The other alternative, if soil is contaminated, is to dig it out to a depth of approximately 15 cm (6 in) and renew it with fresh soil.

In horticulture charcoal performs seven functions; in birdlife it also has many duties. Try to find a burnt-out tree, especially a hollow one — box and coolabah are the best I have found. Over many years the rotting in the centre results in a build up of materials at the base of the tree. This material has been eaten over by insects and ants. In the middle there are also large lumps of what looks like red clay. This is just as important to the diet as the charcoal. Both of these can be collected and crushed (an old meat mincer is ideal for this job)

and stored until required. Old well-rotted leaf mould which has a nice earthy smell, and the inside of rotting logs, will also be appreciated by your birds.

Grit

Grit is important because it grinds and separates the seeds and other foods as they pass through the gizzard. It is an essential aid to digestion.

Today, grit is mostly composed of crushed scallop and oyster shell, some of which has been medicated. If you are fortunate enough to be able to collect some grit on a clean private beach I believe this is much better because it contains such things as calcium, boron, iodine and salt. You can also grind up eggshells to make a grit, but pre-bake them to destroy any harmful ingredients. Cuttle-fish bone is probably the most readily available and best known source of calcium. Old lime mortar (calcium hydroxide) can be obtained off old bricks. This is soft, and easily removed.

Phosphate deficiency in budgerigars is often overlooked because of its availability. The best source of phosphates is sterilised bone meal which also acts as a food-grinding grit.

Rock salt should be available at all times in the aviary. Remember, the redder it is the more iron it contains and therefore the more beneficial it is. Take care in the breeding cabinets though because sometimes the birds can have too much and dehydrate as a result. The manufactured compound block available to livestock generally contains more minerals and in some cases could be of greater benefit to the budgerigars than the imported red rock salt.

In addition, an old softer type of housebrick is useful for the birds to chew at to keep their beaks trim. All the materials from the charcoal to the bone meal can be mixed together and placed in a grit pan and topped up weekly. Some years ago I could purchase a good grit, made by my local Eggboard. Its contents were:

Crushed eggshell (pre-baked)

Ground rock salt

Crushed cooked scallop shell

Iron oxide pre-tested to be compatible with wildlife

Charcoal

A mineral and grit block can be made from the following ingredients, ground up if necessary. Add anything else you desire.

10 parts grit
2 parts bonemeal
3 parts ground charcoal
1 part ground rock salt
1 part ground cuttle bone

Add three parts of the mixture to one part of hydrated lime and a quarter of cement. Mix it all thoroughly, gradually adding the water and mixing to a thick paste. Place in trays, mark into squares and leave to set. You can place a piece of wire, angled at the end so it will not come out of the mixture, into each square so that you can hang it up for use. The block may take up to twenty-one days to set properly. An alternate and preferred method is to use a rock or peanut lime which makes the cement for setting the mixture unnecessary. This method is slightly hazardous however, because the lime, when added to water can make it heat up and boil. Therefore, if using this recipe the paste should be made first and then added to the dry mixture.

When budgerigars are kept in captivity they appear to become cannibals. When one dies the others will quickly scalp it and chew at the rest of it. I believe that birds require a certain amount of meat and fat, although this is usually not available to domesticated birds. For this reason, I supply mine with sheeps' tails or suet which are easily pierced and hung on a nail. I have also seen a dried fish meal used and see no reason why a meat meal could not also be acceptable as a source of nourishment.

Water

Water is becoming an ever-increasing problem for many. In its native environment the budgerigar often drinks where the water is brackish. This is water that is very unpalatable to humans, owing to its high salinity and mineral content. These salts and minerals, which have been leached from the soil in its catchment areas, are beneficial to wildlife and livestock, although they may cause stomach upsets in people who are unaccustomed to them.

Pollution waste and insecticides find their way into many of the catchment regions of our town water supplies too, and as well as these some of us also have to contend with the chemicals added before the water is distributed for our consumption. In some countries fanciers only give their birds water they have boiled. One alternative is to use a rainwater tank, but this is possible only if one is not near industrial areas where there is air pollution. If, however, one is lucky enough to have good well water one should have no problems.

Because diseases are transmitted in the air and by other birds — starlings, doves etc. — an open water container is not advisable and the water bottle system is the preferred method of supplying water in an aviary.

With budgerigars, however, if an open water container is used the main task is to keep the drinking vessels clean. If you use an open vessel that can be contaminated, say from bird droppings, you cannot change the water and clean the vessel too often. Periodically you may put enough Condy's Crystals in their water just to give it a slight colouring to help prevent diseases that are sometimes transmitted through water contamination, but do not overdo it because it is a poison. Use of the water bottle system, described in the chapter, Aviaries, Cages and Appliances, is the best method to reduce infestation and spread of some diseases because it is closed and the water may be used until the bottle is empty. It is also easier to keep clean.

Nevertheless, it is advisable, in very hot weather, to change the water every day as it tends to become warm. If introducing the water bottle system to budgerigars for the first time make the hole a little larger and keep an eye on them until one bird discovers the new drinking method, then the others will soon follow. I have always found this means of giving my birds water to be very satisfactory.

Additives

Some fanciers today must have a cabinet full of wonder mixtures and the only time many birds would obtain pure drinking water would be when they were fortunate enough to get a few raindrops. Needless to say, it is best to alternate mixtures that are added to the drinking water because this lessens the chances of the birds receiving overdoses and increases the benefit. A good tonic such as Parishes Food can be given during moults, especially the one prior to breeding time because the birds experience considerable physical changes at this time.

Lime, added to water prior to and during the laying periods, is a source of calcium, especially necessary if soft or thin-shelled eggs are being laid. This can be made easily by adding a heaped teaspoon of hydrated lime to 4 L (1 gal) of water, shake until dissolved and leave to stand overnight. Pour off the liquid, leaving any sediment behind. I place a clay brick on the floor under my drinking bottle. This traps and solidifies the drips of some solutions for the birds to pick at later.

1

3

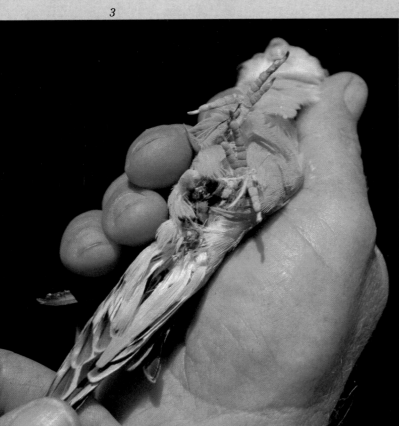

2

4

5 DISEASES AND AILMENTS

Domesticated budgerigars are generally a vigorous healthy lot, however, they do originate from an arid environment and are, therefore, more prone to illnesses and complaints which thrive in damp and humid conditions. They are also susceptible to chills because their feathers do not have the protective wax layers found on the feathers of wild budgerigars.

It is not my aim here to give the veterinary science of the causes and cures of the many ailments to which budgerigars are susceptible because I do not have the knowledge to do so. The average fancier like myself has only a layperson's ability to deal with simple ailments and has to rely upon the mass of literature available. If one reads the books written by veterinary experts one soon becomes aware of the vast number of health problems that can beset budgerigars.

Birds, like humans, do not all respond in the same way to treatment by drugs and too many drugs are given without any knowledge of their effects. Before administering any drugs we should pause and ask the simple question 'Is it useful or is it harmful?' A veterinarian with an expert knowledge of diseases in cage birds is probably best able to answer such a question.

Hygiene

Prevention is better than cure, therefore, hygiene is very important at all times, but particularly when diseases or ailments are apparent. The use of antiseptic and hot water for a thorough scrubdown must pay dividends, even in a pet's cage, although if done every day this will cause more problems than it will solve. Budgerigars are natural pickers and daily cleaning is not advisable. On the other hand, if droppings, husks, feathers and dust are allowed to

1. This bird is showing early signs of illness.

2. Discolouration of facial feathers is a sure sign of discharges from the mouth, nostrils or vent.

3. This bird shows advanced signs of ill-health.

4. French Moult is affecting this six week old youngster.

accumulate to any extent they will certainly cause germs to breed and disease to spread. And, in such an environment of dust and stale air respiratory illness in both birds and humans may result.

Symptoms

Early detection is important in the cure of any ailment: this becomes quite easy for those who have had a long association with budgerigars but to the beginner or the pet owner it is not so easy and many problems will have already reached a very advanced stage before the signs of distress are detected. Nevertheless, there are some symptoms that even the most inexperienced person can readily observe.

When a healthy bird is sleeping with its head under one wing it usually stands on one leg only, but when a bird is ill it tucks its head under one wing, its feathers are ruffled, and both feet are on the perch.

Another sign of illness is when a bird is found huddled up, with its body feathers seemingly straight out and with the vent performing a heavy pumping action. This bird is *very* ill. In addition, the eyes may be dull and half closed and from the mouth or nostrils there may be a mucous discharge which is covering the facial feathers. Also, feathers surrounding the vent may be soiled due to looseness in the droppings and the bird will continually pick and scratch at this area causing its beak to become stained.

Treatment

In the majority of these cases the best cure is complete isolation and warmth combined with the use of a drug.

Of the drugs, two simple choices are available to the uninformed — a sulphur drug or an antibiotic, both of which could help return the sick bird to good health. In today's world the antibiotic is popular and is too readily offered as a be-all and cure-all. Be that as it may, it is more likely that the bird's ailment is one that would respond better to

A heated hospital cage.

the use of a sulphur drug. Therefore, if professional advice is not available and time is an important factor, use a soluble sulphur drug. Proprietary lines now offer for veterinary use a combination of three sulphur drugs and many breeders have had considerable success in the use of these products.

Initially, the triple sulphur solution should be administered by means of a drop or two to the beak of the sick bird. Consequent treatment should then follow the instructions, that is, so many drops per 100 ml of drinking water.

If after a few days the bird is still alive but has not shown any noticeable response to the treatment then it is worthwhile switching to the antibiotic. The various 'mycins' are available in soluble form in 250-500 mg capsules. One capsule of 500 mg dissolved in 600 ml of water should be quite effective.

The duration of any treatment will vary according to the severity of the illness. Those that appear suddenly and severely require less time to cure but a chronic infection may have to be treated for a longer period.

You may wonder why there has not been an endeavour to nominate what illness or disease has beset our sick birds. The answer is quite simple: without professional advice it is not possible to accurately diagnose and treat an illness. Nevertheless, the need to act quickly often prevents one from seeking professional attention because there is often very little time between early signs of distress and a dead bird. Thus, the above comments are based on a layperson's experiences in

restoring a valued specimen to good health. In practice, these methods have given a measure of success.

Application of heat

When heat is applied to a sick budgerigar it is wonderful to see how rapidly they recover. Hospital cages (described in the chapter, Aviaries, Cages and Appliances) are ideal for this because the sick bird can be placed inside and the heat increased gradually until it reaches 32°C (90°F). Alternatively, one can improvise, by suspending a 40 watt light bulb in front of a cage. Cover the cage and light, although not completely, with a heavy cloth or bag in order to retain the heat. It is also advisable to place a cloth on the cage floor — this will increase the comfort of the bird. When the bird has recovered, a gradual cooling-off should take place. This will last longer in cold or winter climates.

Light, heat and some substances such as iron in metal containers can cause deterioration in medications. For these reasons it is advisable to use a dark coloured glass container to supply the medicine, and to top it up constantly, especially if heat is being applied.

Always make sure sick birds have their favourite seeds and perhaps some titbits to entice them to eat — otherwise they will quickly die. And, remember that greenfoods must be withheld because many of these have a purging effect.

I think it appropriate here to dwell on several lessons learnt from a study of the behaviour of obviously sick parrots in their natural state. In the wild sick birds are usually found alone, an indication that they are given complete isolation from any other members of their group. Also, I have noticed that a sick and isolated bird will frequent a burnt-out tree in which, throughout the day, they will continually pick amongst the charcoal and dirt so that by nightfall their crops must be full of these substances. Sometimes they are seen for two or three days before they disappear, whether cured or not I am not certain, although this treatment must be beneficial because it has been noticed too often not to be otherwise. That being so, if you have granulated charcoal available, mix it with grit so the sick bird may derive some benefit from it. In fact, from the point of view of prevention, it is wise to supply birds with this mixture at all times.

Tonics

Tonics may be administered, preferably on alternate days, after the birds have had a severe setback, although the continual use of such products is unwise even in ailing birds, because it acts only as a crutch. In most cases deficiencies are revealed by the birds' behaviour and outward appearance and when this is the case it should be dealt with. If one wishes, there are available many natural sources of vitamins and minerals for birds or, alternatively, one may choose to supplement the deficiency by using one of the many proprietary lines available. Even so, be cautious when using these products, especially fish oils, because an over supply of vitamins, especially in the early development of youngsters, can cause problems.

Internal parasites

Any infestation of worms in budgerigars will be largely a result of the conditions in which they are kept. As a rule, the presence of these parasites is, initially, a result of the droppings of wild birds,

A ring cutter made from a pair of scissors.

which contaminate the soil in cages and aviaries. Although outbreaks can occur in aviaries the presence of worms in pet budgies would be unusual.

Round worm infestation, which appears to be most common, can be effectively controlled with a solution of piperazine citrate, preferably mixed with water. Manufactured preparations available should be used in strict accordance with the manufacturer's directions.

External parasites

As far as lice and mites are concerned the treatment is now very simple. In contrast to the olden times when each bird had to be caught and hand dusted, the modern pressure pack spray allows a tedious job to be reduced to the utmost simplicity. However, it is of paramount importance that the insecticide spray that is used be one that is known to be safe. I have had no problem in the direct spraying of birds with a spray that contains pyrethrins and their allied boosters. The haphazard use of many pressure pack insecticide sprays would be fatal to the birds because some that are used for household purposes contain benzene hexachloride. When severe attacks of red mite are experienced the painting or spraying of kerosene (paraffin) into cracks or crevices may be warranted.

Scale

This is a most common problem affecting budgerigars. The appearance of this beige-coloured crusty deposit is caused by burrowing mites which tunnel through the surface of the skin. When the scale is examined it appears honeycombed and not unlike coral. Scale generally commences in the folded skin between and around the beak and cere, from where it will gradually spread. The eye can become infected, as can the scaled parts of the legs and feet.

In order to treat scale, paint the affected areas with a mixture containing equal parts of an antiseptic, such as Dettol, and olive or castor oil. Leave for a day and then scrape away the scale. Repeat until scale disappears. If the scale has imbedded itself under the leg ring causing a large swelling so that the ring cannot be moved try to work some pure antiseptic into the affected area. If the swelling has not reduced by the next day it will be necessary to remove the ring.

Cutting an aluminium ring off a bird's leg is difficult enough, however, when a leg is swollen so that the flesh exudes both below and above the ring it is a somewhat terrifying task. Originally, we used a very small three-cornered file to file through the ring, which was held firmly in a pair of pliers. It was necessary to file half way through the ring on one side, then on the opposite side, completely through. This allowed the ring to be parted and removed. It is a satisfactory method but it does take two people 15-20 minutes to complete. A much faster and more efficient way has been devised by the use of a modified pair of sewing scissors; these are very difficult to describe but the photograph on page 49 shows the modification. Using these scissors, it takes only three or four seconds to gently cut through the ring. Because of the angle of the scissor blades only one cut is

Apply the scale mixture as shown. As a further precaution, apply the mixture to the skin area surrounding the beak and feet.

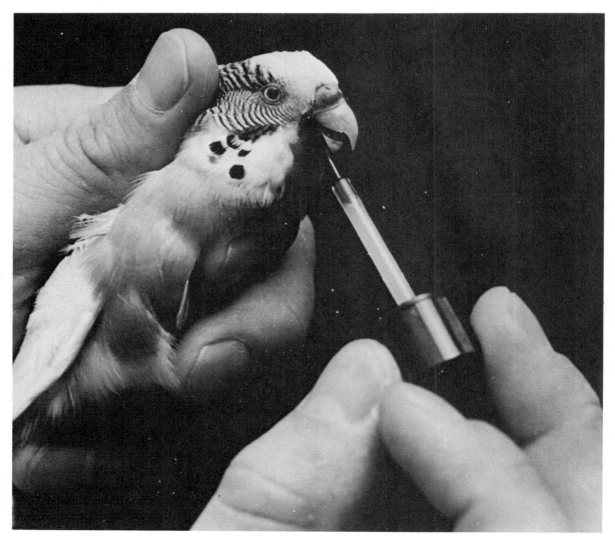

needed to spring the ring apart, and the bird suffers no discomfort whatsoever.

Legs

The disability caused by splayed legs can be remedied if it is detected in the early stage in the nest box. Both legs should be drawn together a little closer than normal with a small piece of fine cord (not sewing thread). Tie just above the claws. This restrictive cord, or hobble, can be removed after four days when the legs should remain in their normal position.

Feet

If a bird suffers from paralysis in the legs place it on its back and, while rubbing warm oil (castor or olive oil) into the legs, massage and exercise them bicycle fashion for about ten minutes. Do this twice a day. It may take up to a week before the feet are back to normal.

Although good results occur with this treatment, a bird may not always respond.

Mice

Mice are more of a problem than one would think because sickness can result from the presence of their urine in the bird's food. Eradication is necessary and if poisons are used in large cages and aviaries these should be put in a small cage that is placed under a box with holes large enough for the mice to enter. The same procedure can be carried out using traps.

Parrot's disease

A warning to all budgerigar owners: *Psittacosis* or *Ornithosis*, an infectious disease of parrots, can be transmitted to human beings. The disease is not common when you consider the number of people who keep budgerigars, however, pet owners especially should be warned that a friendly peck could prove fatal if the pet has this disease.

Beak malformations

Since breeding in captivity commenced, the top beak (mandible) of a budgerigar has been altered from a long bill to a hooked bill. This change has also resulted in an ailment commonly called *undershot beak*. This problem originates in youngsters in the nest. It is caused by food caught under the soft hook of the upper mandible. If regular cleaning is not carried out the food acts like a plaster cast, causing the hook to turn under so that the beak eventually passes under the bottom mandible rather than over it.

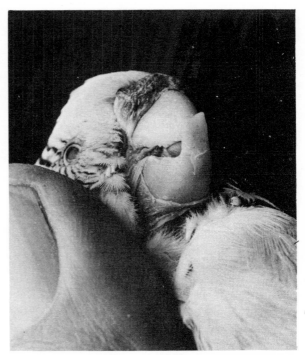

This bird's undershot beak should be trimmed for easier feeding. (See page 37 for trimming instructions.)

To correct any beak malformation the best practice is to cut both beaks. Concave nail clippers are ideal for this job but always take care to avoid cutting the vein. After cutting, the filing of both beaks may be necessary for them to overlap correctly. This procedure is not always effective and periodical trimmings may be necessary.

Egg binding

The detection of an egg-bound hen can be very distressing. Often these hens will be seen trying to expel the often visible egg on the cage or aviary floor while other hens will be standing in a corner of the nest box, their now cold eggs scattered by the distraught bird. Regardless of whether the egg is visible or not the area around the vent will appear heavy and inflamed and a gentle examination with your fingers will usually confirm the diagnosis of an egg-bound hen. There are two forms of this ailment: hard shell and soft shell. Of the two, the latter is invariably the worst, although both cases will quickly prove fatal if not dealt with immediately.

One method of treatment is to warm some castor oil (more soothing than olive oil) and with a feather paint it on the hen's vent, which should be pointing upwards. This allows the oil to be taken internally as the contractions take place. In addition, a few drops placed into the beak will do no harm and hopefully, with the application of heat, the hen may eventually expel the egg.

Manipulating the egg with your fingers with the help of the contractions by the hen is practised by some breeders with success, but this is only possible in the early period of egg-binding. And if, due to inexperience, the egg is broken internally, this may cause, among other things, septicaemia.

While the above methods are more commonly used and perhaps, more acceptable to the reader, there is another technique, which is far more effective. Again, hold the affected bird in the hand so that the vent is uppermost. Shake salt from a salt pot so the grains fall on the vent area: the immediate result is a contraction — just what is required. A little more salt should be sprinkled on the affected area and the bird placed in a comfortable spot where the egg should shortly be laid.

Moults

Budgerigars moult at irregular times although adults have at least one main moult a year which generally occurs in the autumn months. Minor forms of coat changing are very erratic, particularly in pet budgies which are continually subjected to varying conditions.

Although moulting is a natural process it can become an ailment if a bird's physical condition deteriorates. When a bird is unable to complete the moult, its health will deteriorate and it will die.

Another associated complaint is when birds chew to shreds the quills of moulted feathers in an effort to derive some benefit from them. In some extreme cases birds will even pull out the new feathers of other birds, especially around the tail and oil gland, and chew them, often while blood is oozing from the quill.

To alleviate and prevent these nutritional deficiencies a tonic or additives containing a quantity of phosphate and calcium should be included with a well-balanced diet during all moulting periods.

French Moult

The appearance of French Moult in budgerigars was first recorded in about 1880 in France and since this early period it has commonly occurred in African love birds.

Many breeders, including myself, have bred *runners* (the breeder's term for birds suffering from French Moult). In advanced cases of this complaint birds leave the nest practically naked, with no hope of the feathers ever growing. For humane reasons these poor unfortunate birds should be destroyed.

In other cases when only some of the tail and flight feathers drop out (including the quill butts), these birds will generally regrow their full complement of feathers after leaving the box. A further example is when there is continual bleeding at the stumps with only an odd flight feather regrowing; these birds will never fly.

There is virtually no reliable explanation of the causes and possible cures of this condition. My own personal opinion is that there are various causes, some of which have also been expounded by other breeders. I shall not expound those views here, instead I shall leave some food for thought.

Firstly, when half the eggs from a pair producing French Moult are transferred to another establishment where the complaint is not evident and are placed and hatched under a foster pair together with eggs of their own, the results have been that the young from these eggs remain French Moulters, while the foster pair's young, which were hatched in the same nest, are all normally feathered birds. In this case this disproves the theory that incorrect feeding by the parents is responsible for French Moult.

Secondly, there is also the evidence of a friend in England. He had two hens that were unable to fly: for six months they had climbed the wire and run over the aviary floor. For an experiment, he placed one hen in an outside breeding flight. Within four weeks her feathers had grown enough for her to fly and she then laid and produced all normal healthy youngsters. The same results were experienced with the other hen, and when I saw these hens rearing their second broods there was no evidence of their prior disabilities.

Thirdly, the beak attributes its origin to the same source as the feathers, yet I have never noticed problems relating to the beak in birds suffering from French Moult.

To my knowledge no positive proof has been observed concerning French Moult in wild budgerigars but a recent find in western New South Wales may prove it could occur. Two small boys noticed a young Red Rump (Grass Parrot) near a water hole and as they approached the bird it became evident it was unable to fly. After catching the parrot they passed it into the hands of a budgerigar breeder in a nearby town.

On inspecting the wings it became quite apparent these were suffering from a feather loss. From this and later observations of the feathers that continued to fall out he was convinced this wild fledging was suffering from French Moult.

6 AVIARIES, CAGES AND APPLIANCES

Cost and the availability of space were the sole two determining factors affecting the construction of aviaries in the past. Today, however, with new laws implemented in many places, we have to consider such things as noise pollution and permission to build from a local authority. Wildlife organisations, too, administer cage sizes and conditions, and the number of birds to be kept in them.

The keeping and breeding of budgerigars can only be successfully accomplished when the environment in which they are kept is satisfactory. Where numbers are to be kept, an aviary is essential, although beginners will often start out with a small box or breeding cage built on the same lines as the professional individual breeding cages. In time, because budgerigars are prolific breeders, this type of housing will soon become overcrowded.

A structure, built to house budgerigars, should include a shelter shed at the back and wire flights at the front. Specialist breeders would also have a division in the centre to separate cocks from hens. The aim of this chapter is to provide specifications for constructing structures for one's hobby. These can be modified according to the materials one has on hand. A general rule, however, is that more length than breadth is advisable in the floor plan to ensure adequate space for the birds to exercise as shown in Figure 6.0. An indication of aviary size is that 150 budgerigars can be comfortably housed in an area of 3 m x 1.8 m (10 ft x 6 ft).

As there are no hard and fast rules tastes vary from a disused shed with a wire front, to elaborate establishments built by tradesmen. For the handy person there are excellent designs available which provide detailed specifications that can be followed easily.

The positioning of your cage or aviary is very important. The best aspect is a site where birds are sheltered from the cold winds and rain. In addition, there should always be adequate sunshine. Sleeping quarters must be free of draughts so care should be taken during construction to ensure that the smallest cracks or holes are excluded. In some areas it will be advisable to completely enclose these

A well established and well located aviary.

A compartment aviary incorporating a covered flight area.

quarters and in others an efficient windbreak may be all that is necessary.

The roof should be watertight, with enough fall to prevent rainfall overflow or damage by snow. In cold or hot areas it should be insulated — when fibreglass is used you must always remember that it is 5°C (8°F) hotter than glass sheeting. In all constructions remember budgerigars are more susceptible to problems from the heat than from the cold. Therefore, in the areas where extreme heat sometimes prevails, it may be advisable to provide a water sprinkler system on the roof.

Preservation of outside timber in aviaries with paint or oil is beneficial, especially in areas that are subject to the weather — this should be done before the wire is fitted. White and pale coloured paints are cooler and reflect more light, but regardless of your choice in this matter, one should take care that the paint is non-toxic otherwise it will be detrimental to the birds. Paints which give a Spanish-style textured finish generally reduce the inside temperature on hot days enormously when applied to any outside surface or roofing material.

If one uses lights a dimmer, with or without an automatic time switch, will be needed. Of course, in countries where daylight hours are short during the breeding season, this will be an essential feature.

The door into the aviary, cage or birdroom should be properly locked to prevent the entry of any intruder. The choice of a lock especially designed for the style of door you have is very important.

Site

Before commencing construction you should have a well-thought out plan of your present and future needs. If you are planning to move your aviary to another address, or even to extend it in any

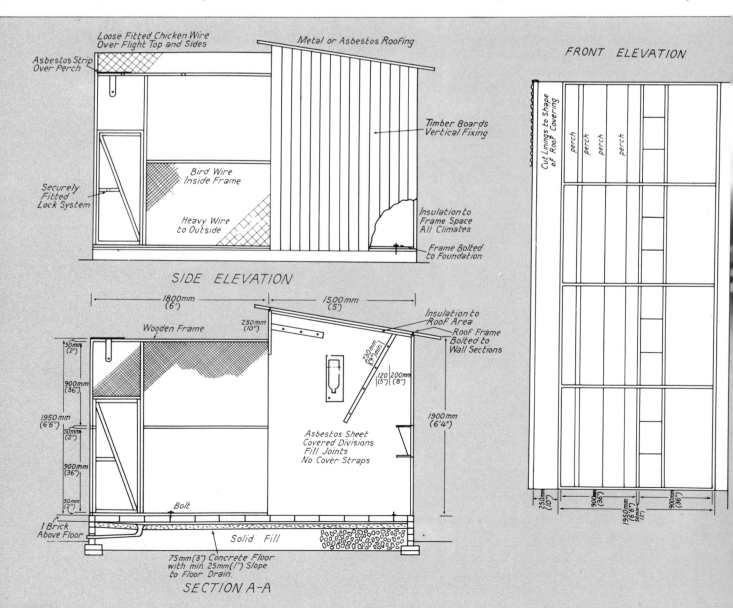

direction at some later date, take this into consideration. Where there are damp areas, these should be drained and built up before any attempt is made to build on them. Surrounding trees also have to be taken into account because these may present problems with falling limbs later. Of course, if only a portable cage is being made these problems will not arise.

The small cage shown in Figure 6.1 is mounted on legs, raising it well above ground level to guard against domestic predators. Furthermore, it may be necessary to bury a brick under each leg to make the structure more stable. A wise precaution is to hinge the door from the top of the cage to prevent it from being left open.

In portable cages and aviaries where box type or circular construction is used, the roof should be designed and one perch located so that the birds can have complete seclusion if they wish.

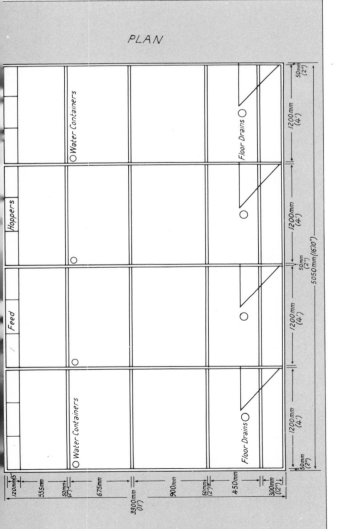

PLAN

Building Materials

The use of cement (fibro) sheeting for the shelter is not recommended because, in most instances, it is prone to easy breakage; on the other hand, if softwood cladding is used, a small knot will quickly be gnawed into a hole through which birds could escape. Lead should never be used in any construction either because if the birds chew it they will quickly succumb with lead poisoning.

On the open flights double wire is recommended, that is, wire on the inside and outside of the studs. This is to prevent cats and rats from climbing up the wire and biting the birds' feet, especially at night. Also, on the bottom of open flights it may be advisable to use a heavy chain wire mesh for your outer wire. This will prevent dogs from biting holes in the wire, forcing their entry, and killing your birds. An occurrence, unfortunately, quite common.

Mice are also a problem and can gain entry even when 9.5 mm (⅜ in) birdwire is used — only fine gauze or fly wire will keep them out. It is also a sound practice to extend a wire frame above the outside flights. This is best done by extending the corner uprights (studs) 450 mm (18 in). Thread a heavy gauge plain wire through holes drilled near the top and tighten to form a frame. Place 50 mm (2 in) chicken wire over the top — this will eliminate prowling cats.

To extend a small outside flight loft a steel frame can be bolted through the corner studs of the existing frame and enclosed with weld mesh or wire. A timber aviary, however, is not as simple to extend and allowances for increased size should be made in the original design.

Construction

The first step, when building, is to set out the length and breadth correctly. Then the site should be squared by measuring diagonally from the bottom left hand corner to the top right hand corner and vice versa — this will pay dividends when you come to erect and line the roof.

A brick foundation, well above ground level, will be necessary if one is having a concrete floor. Many breeders prefer a concrete floor throughout the entire aviary because it is the only way to eliminate rats. It also helps to eliminate disease because it can be thoroughly cleaned and dirt and grit which are spread over the area can be easily removed when contaminated.

Figure 6.0 An aviary plan incorporating four separate compartments with an open flight area.

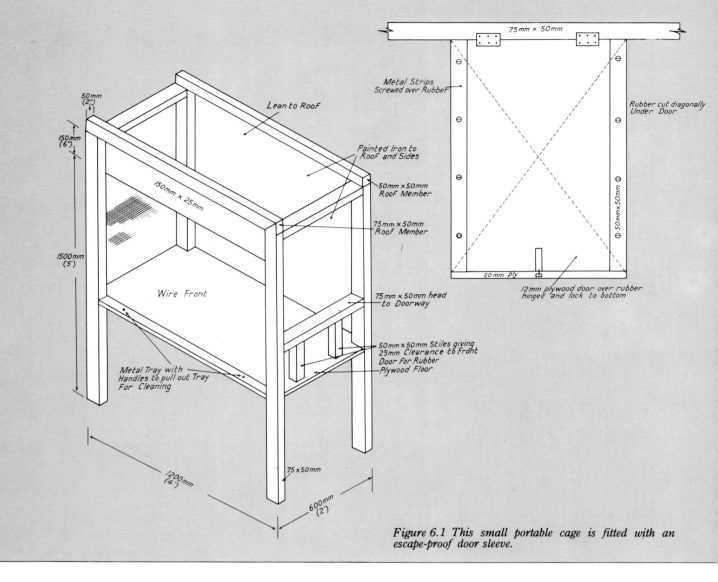

Figure 6.1 *This small portable cage is fitted with an escape-proof door sleeve.*

Labels on the diagrams:

50mm (2")
150mm (6")
1500mm (5')
150mm x 25mm
Wire Front
Lean to Roof
Painted Iron to Roof and Sides
50mm x 50mm Roof Member
75mm x 50mm Roof Member
75mm x 50mm head to Doorway
50mm x 50mm Stiles giving 25mm Clearance to Front Door for Rubber
Plywood Floor
Metal Tray with Handles to pull out Tray For Cleaning
1200mm (4')
75 x 50mm
600mm (2')

75 mm x 50mm
Metal Strips Screwed over Rubber
Rubber cut diagonally Under Door
50mm x 50mm
20 mm Ply
12 mm plywood door over rubber hinged and lock to bottom

For good drainage the floor should have a fall of 25 mm (1 in) and include a drainage trap that excludes mice. Bolts should be imbedded into the concrete so that the framework can be bolted down. In areas of high wind an added precaution would be to also have 9.5 mm (⅜ in) steel rods bent at right angles set into the concrete floor: these should be long enough to facilitate the bolting down of the roof timber. Always skew (angle) the nails when securing roofing materials.

It is a sound practice to lay one course of brickwork on the concrete floor where the aviary structure is to be positioned. This preventative measure will help prevent the rotting out of the bottom section of the frame.

Aviary framing is mainly intended to support sheets of cladding or wire netting, which may be run vertical or horizontal. Therefore, the distance between the stud centres will have to suit the size of the materials you intend to use. When narrow wire netting is used it is best placed on horizontal framing. To do this, first secure the wire netting at one end with staples, then slowly progress to each corner, pulling it taut and fixing it to the frame as you go.

If the remainder of the sides and rear are to be weatherboarded and lined for colder climates, insulation such as fibreglass should be installed between the linings. Any galvanised iron used as external cladding on walls and roof should be painted on both sides if the aviary is not to be lined or insulated.

Aviary doors should be about 1.2 m (4 ft) high, that is, a height that is lower than the ceiling. This allows easy access but reduces the risk of the birds escaping. The door is best situated in the wire

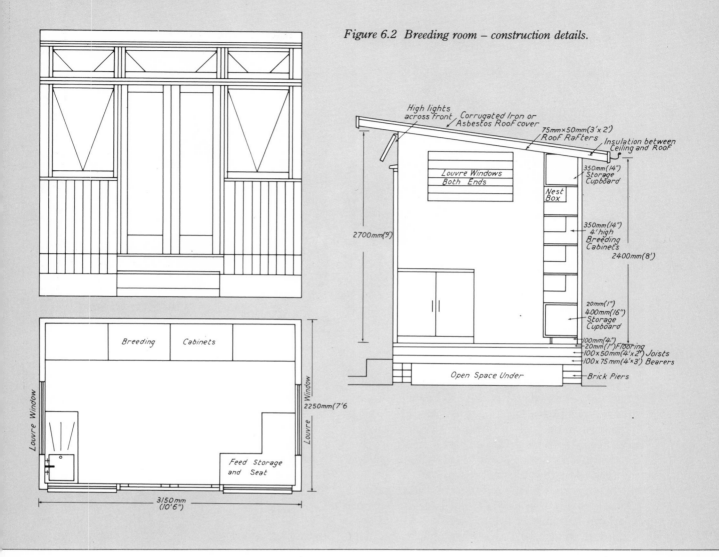

Figure 6.2 Breeding room – construction details.

High lights across front, Corrugated Iron or Asbestos Roof cover
75mm×50mm(3'x 2') Roof Rafters
Insulation between Ceiling and Roof
Louvre Windows Both Ends
Nest Box
350mm(14") Storage Cupboard
350mm(14") 4' high Breeding Cabinets
2400mm(8')
2700mm(9')
20mm(1")
400mm(16") Storage Cupboard
100mm(4")
20mm(1")Flooring
100×50mm(4'x2') Joists
100×75mm(4'x3') Bearers
Open Space Under
Brick Piers

Breeding *Cabinets*
Louvre Window
Louvre Window
2250mm(7'6
Feed Storage and Seat
3150 mm (10'6")

flights to allow the birds to see people entering.

Perches

Perches should be located in both the flight area and the sheltered area. In the former, one or two perches high up would be sufficient; in the sheltered area sets of perches to suit the number of birds housed may be attached 230 mm (9 in) apart on a runner at each end. These should then be fastened close to the back wall in an almost vertical position, thus giving a larger exercise area. Perches placed close to the roof in the enclosed area at the front of the shelter will provide some protection from strong winds.

The provision of square or rounded perches in any hardwood material will alleviate their constant renewal. These may vary from 9.5 mm (⅜ in) to 19 mm (¾ in) in diameter.

Birdrooms

A birdroom, whether it be for the professional breeder or the person who keeps budgerigars as a hobby, does not have to be elaborate — just comfortable and efficient. Most breeders, however, get a lot of personal satisfaction out of the construction and outfitting of their birdrooms particularly because, in many instances, the building of the birdroom is the first step of the hobby. Later, the fancier may add flights to the birdroom, thereby converting it to an aviary or combined aviary and birdroom. If flights are added at each end, the result is a large U-shaped building with a courtyard in which one can sit and while away the hours, watching the performances of one's birds.

Light and fresh air are essential in any birdroom and yours should be planned accordingly, for

A drawer-type nest box which slides into the cage.

Part of a breeding unit showing the drawer-type nest boxes.

example, in Figure 6.2 good cross ventilation is provided by small adjustable louvred windows at each end of the room; at the front an abundance of natural ventilation and light is also provided by windows and a door. If one also has electricity one can install an electrical extractor fan, or alternatively, a wind-driven rotor vent — both will draw out any dust that accumulates.

Screens should be fitted to all openings, including highlights at the front of the building. In addition, a flap can be made of light material and hung inside the door to avoid escapes when opening the door.

There are many prefabricated sheds and garages that are easily transformed into a comfortable birdroom. The suitability of any building will depend entirely on the number of cages you wish to use — a 3 m (10 ft) inside measurement will comfortably take four breeding cages lengthways. The breadth of the birdroom would have to be a minimum of 1.8 m (6 ft) to allow for a sink with a regulated water point at one end. An ideal height for the birdroom would be 2.7 m (9 ft) at the front and sloping to 2.4 m (8 ft) at the rear. The extra height in the front allows the installation of highlights which provide extra light and ventilation and facilitates later extensions or the addition of an aviary.

If outside flights are constructed against the birdroom they should be closed off so that the problem of draughts is avoided.

After the breeding cages have been placed either on a cupboard or stand, the area above them can be utilised for storage. In addition, a narrow cupboard

over the sink is handy for small incidentals including medicines. A training cage to place your youngsters in after they have been taken from the breeding cage is essential and planning should allow for its positioning.

Seed holding bins can be installed under the windows or against flight walls, but should be well above floor level to prevent moisture from affecting the seed.

Breeding cages

Breeding cages are positioned off the floor, perhaps with a cupboard approximately 330 mm (13 in) high underneath to enable storage of equipment such as show cages. Although most breeders have their own ideas on what size a breeding cage should be, a recommended size would be 760 mm (2 ft 6 in) long x 380 mm (15 in) high x 406 mm (16 in) deep. These may be built individually or in blocks of units with sliding partitions installed so that they can be readily converted for use as holding cages. In the cabinets illustrated above, the nest boxes are inside the cage and can be slid in and out to provide quick and easy inspection.

Breeding cages can be constructed from chipboard or plywood. A compact unit of cages can also be made from a disused double wardrobe — remove the doors and any partitioning and insert three horizontal shelves and a divider in the centre. After the addition of the cage fronts, together with two different-sized perches and appropriate nest boxes, one will have a bank of eight units. To

A sliding divider regulates the size of the cage.

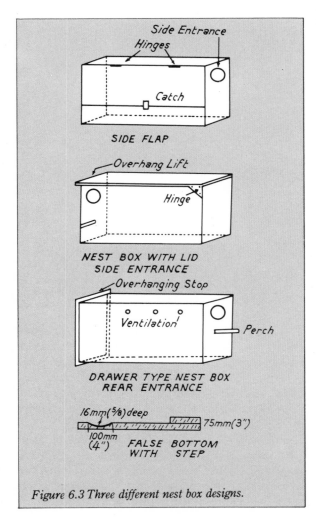

Side Entrance
Hinges
Catch

SIDE FLAP

Overhang Lift
Hinge

NEST BOX WITH LID
SIDE ENTRANCE

Overhanging Stop
Ventilation
Perch

DRAWER TYPE NEST BOX
REAR ENTRANCE

16mm (⅝) deep   75mm (3")
100mm
(4")   FALSE BOTTOM
WITH STEP

Figure 6.3 Three different nest box designs.

facilitate easy cleaning a space of 19 mm (¾ in) can be allowed at the bottom of the cage to take a galvanised iron, sliding, floor tray. Apply a good gloss paint to them to aid cleaning and give a pleasing appearance.

Punch bar or welded wire cage fronts are preferred on breeding cages, especially when they incorporate a lift-up or swinging door. Always make sure the door is large enough for the utensils and nests to be passed through. If one wishes to install a slide-in nest box a slight modification will be necessary: cut a hole in the top left or right hand corner to take the nest box — allow an extra 19 mm (¾ in) in height. Rebate a 25 mm (1 in) piece of timber to fit tightly over the tops of the cut bars, then attach a 25 mm x 25 mm (1 in x 1 in) T-shaped support, to be fixed in a horizontal position to the rear of the cage, for the box to rest on. This will also serve as a perch when the birds come out of the nest box.

Nest boxes

There are a wide variety of nest boxes. Some are fashioned to hook onto the outside of a cage and others are hung and supported by various means on the inside. The most efficient of all, however, is the slide-in nest box which allows a quick look from above, thus enabling one to see the eggs and young more clearly and, if necessary, to remove the nest box altogether for further inspection.

Although lids are not absolutely necessary when the nest box fits close to the top of the cage, some method of seeing into the nest box has to be devised when nests are completely enclosed in the breeding cage. For this reason, some boxes have a lid on hinges at one end. These can be simply made from two three-cornered flat pieces of metal, each fixed by two nails to the lid and one to the box as shown in Figure 6.3.

Others are designed with a flap which opens out on two butt hinges on one side of the nest: others have a simple slide at one end. Both types give one a limited view of eggs and young with advanced youngsters often escaping or falling out during the inspection.

A good-sized nest box will vary in length but will be 250 mm (10 in) high and 200 mm (8 in) wide with an entrance hole 50 mm (2 in) in diameter placed high up at one end. Waterproof ply can be used for their manufacture although solid wood at both ends is advisable. Small ventilation holes should then be added at the top of the nest so that there is no build-up of moisture inside. Although not absolutely

A nest box designed to fit outside the cage.

necessary, a removable bottom with a concave at the end furthest from the entrance hole is preferred by some breeders. The concave helps to prevent the eggs from scattering and the hen from squashing the chicks. At the opposite end, near the entrance hole, a soft timber step can be added for the hen to gnaw at so that she does not damage or destroy the nest box.

Appliances for cage and aviary

There are many feeding and watering utensils for sale, most of which are smaller or larger versions of open receptacles. These require daily replenishment. The preferred utensils are the automatic seed hoppers, which alleviate the problem of the scattering and fouling of seed. They should not, of course, be placed beneath perches and must at all times be protected from the weather. The best place for them is on a cladded side of the cage or aviary and approximately 900 mm (3 ft) off the floor. This minimises the problem of startled birds flying upwards and colliding with the hopper base.

The birds should pick out their seed close to the clear glass front, which should be fixed so that it is sloping outwards from a point 19 mm (¾ in) above the hopper floor. If this is the case the seed will slide on the glass and not be obstructed or clogged.

Seed hopper

Working drawings for the construction of a seed hopper for a large aviary are provided in Figure 6.4.

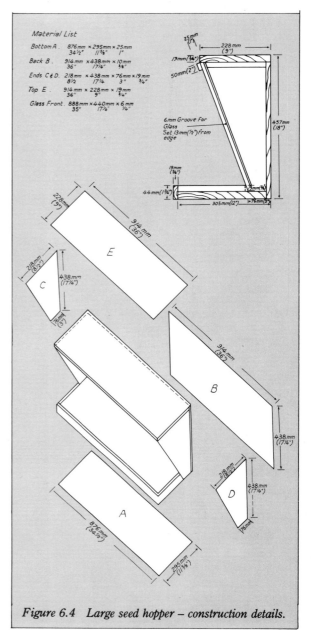

Figure 6.4   Large seed hopper – construction details.

This seed hopper holds 45 L (10 gal) of seed, allows twenty-five birds to feed at one time, and is suitable for an aviary of 200 birds. One practical tip when constructing a seed hopper, is to first butt each piece together before fastening them into place. This way adjustments can be made to the grooves for the glass before it is all put together.

Small self-feeders in Figure 6.5 can also be made with dual compartments to separate different seeds. These are constructed on square lines and have a false sloping back inserted to enable the seed to slide forward. Another self-feeder is

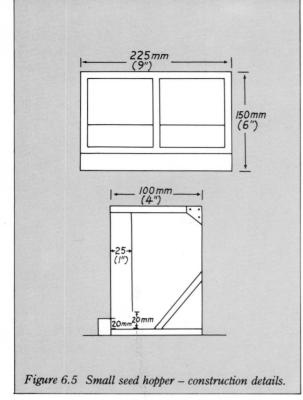

Figure 6.5 Small seed hopper – construction details.

A small seed hopper.

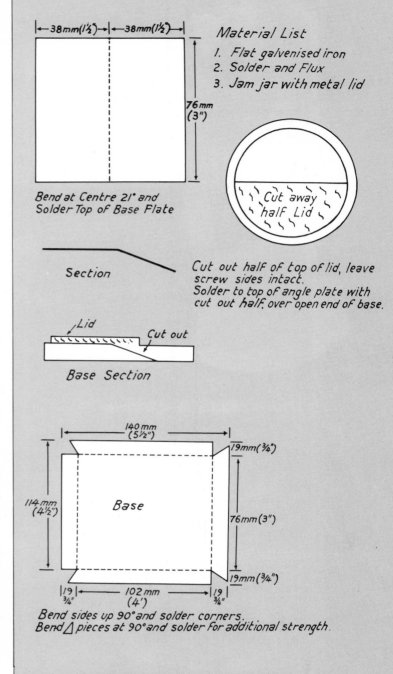

Material List

1. Flat galvenised iron
2. Solder and Flux
3. Jam jar with metal lid

38mm (1½) 38mm (1½)

76 mm (3")

Bend at Centre 21° and
Solder Top of Base Plate

Cut away half Lid

Section

Cut out half of top of lid, leave
screw sides intact.
Solder to top of angle plate with
cut out half, over open end of base.

Lid   Cut out

Base Section

140 mm (5½")

19mm (¾")

114 mm (4½")   Base   76mm (3")

19mm (¾")

19 ¾   102 mm (4')   19 ¾

Bend sides up 90° and solder corners.
Bend △ pieces at 90° and solder for additional strength.

Figure 6.6 Base for jar-type feeder – construction details.

illustrated in Figure 6.6. It is easily made with a screw-top jar.

Water utensils

Drinking water in cages and aviaries is best provided by an upturned clear bottle (self-waterer). Some are fitted at the outlet with an open font but the best method is simply to use a screw cap with a 5 mm (³/₁₆ in) hole drilled in the centre — a plastic cap or salt-shaker top would be ideal.

For small cages square-faced bottles are preferred because these fit flush and stable against the wire front when hung, thus avoiding excess movement. Figure 6.7 illustrates how bottles can be secured in position by a simply-made hook: to fasten the hook to the bottle first prepare both surfaces by roughening them with coarse sandpaper, or on an emery wheel. Then use a waterproof adhesive to attach the hook to the bottle. For the larger aviary these drinkers can be made by using any large soft drink bottle with a screw-cap. The timber backing which forms the base of the cradle can be easily screwed into position on the aviary wall.

An open font drinker.

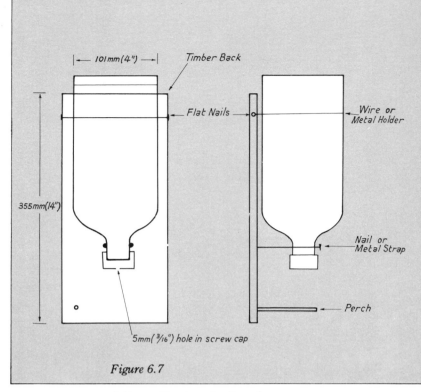

Figure 6.7

Labels in figure: 101mm (4"), Timber Back, Flat Nails, 355mm (14"), 5mm (³/₁₆") hole in screw cap, Wire or Metal Holder, Nail or Metal Strap, Perch

A large self-waterer for the aviary.

Extra items for aviaries

There are excellent sundries that can be purchased: special gripper catches for holding cuttlebone and other titbits; large clips for holding greenfoods; and small plastic finger drawers or the larger open containers, invaluable for holding grits and other special dry mixtures.

For the innumerable cleaning jobs one requires many implements. Scrapers, for example, are indispensible: choose one from the comprehensive painters' range or cut one out of a piece of metal guttering, using the rib section for a grip.

Scouring pads and stiff bottle brushes are also necessary for thorough cleaning of open dishes and water bottles. Another purchase, important for personal health reasons, would be a face mask.

Catching nets

These resemble a butterfly net but have a short handle. They should be made of light cotton material which forms a pad on the narrow rim that is attached to the handle. A useful all-round size is one that is 305 mm (12 in) in diameter and 457 mm (18 in) deep. Like a butterfly net, too, they are tapered at the end.

Carrying cages

A small oblong carrying cage can be made with odds and ends of suitable building material. The cage front may have a long narrow — 50 mm (2 in) — opening near the top of the cage, which can be covered with bird wire or gauze and held in place by

A jar-type feeder, dismantled and filled with seed ready for use.

Hospital cages, where heat is supplied, are invaluable in restoring birds to health and can also be used for drying cages.

some moulding. A round hinged door can be fitted at one end. An extra safety precaution is to fix a flexible rubber mat cut across both diagonals to the inside of the cage. This covers the entire entrance and is attached at the sides. When one wishes to put one's arm into the cage the rubber pieces form a glove around the arm which prevents the bird from escaping.

Hospital cage

The hospital cage, illustrated above and on page 48, is a most useful piece of equipment. This cage is 406 mm (16 in) long, 304 mm (12 in) high and 178 mm (6 in) deep. It is equipped with a thermostatically controlled heating coil. An alternative method of heating can be provided for a hospital cage by incorporating a dimmer switch into the wiring of one or two light globes thus enabling the regulation of the temperature. The globe sockets with a screwed flange are best for this purpose. When mounted on a base the threaded end should be passed through a neat circular hole at one end of the heat box. This will enable the flange nut to be screwed up to hold the unit securely in place. This method has two advantages: firstly, it enables the sockets to be removed easily when washing the cage. Secondly, it allows a sick bird to find comfort at the other end of the cage (away from the light globe), which is not subjected to the same amount of heat.

Hospital cages require constant washing and disinfecting and for this reason it is necessary to use the more durable waterproof ply and glue in their construction.

The hospital cage consists of two chambers. The bottom chamber forms the heatbox and should be lined with aluminium foil to radiate the heat more efficiently. It is separated from the top chamber by two shelves 9.5 mm (⅜ in) apart: the first made of perforated zinc or any stiffened metal covering; the second made of punch bar or a wire mesh. It might be advisable to cover the wire mesh with a piece of towelling because it could become too warm for the bird to stand on.

In the top chamber (sick bay), the perches are fitted on the back of the cage together with an aquarium thermometer. Detachable seed and water containers should also be mounted at the back, although the water should be placed well away from the electrical wiring. The sliding glass front should have a gap of 6 mm (¼ in) at the top to allow for ventilation. A final touch would be to fit a door with an outside flap to minimise heat loss.

This simple loft-type flight will prove advantageous in many ways.

7 BREEDING CARE AND MANAGEMENT

Management

The actual breeding programme begins when the first records of an actual family of birds are made. This keeping of accurate records is most important, for example, if ever a mutation is produced these records will enable the breeder to trace its pedigree and increase its number in a shorter time. On the other hand, if a faulty or a superior bird is evident it will be possible to trace its history in order to eliminate or consolidate those features.

Some breeders have filing card systems that enable them to make efficient checks and references. In addition to one of the many breeding registers available a breeder may also use an exercise book ruled up to his or her requirements. Regardless of which system is used one can also pin a card on each nest box for on-the-spot recording.

Records

A typical breeding record for a pair should read:

Pair or nest No. 7 **Nest taken** 1 only
Cock Light Green s/ Cinn. **Ring No.** BS.80.742
Hen Light Green **Ring No.** BS.79.7490
Date paired 1-6-81
First egg 12-6-81 **Date hatched** 1-7-81
No. of eggs laid 7 **No. hatched** 5
Remarks No. 4 egg clear, No. 7 dead in shell

Ring No.	Variety, Colour, Sex	Remarks
1740	Green cock	Heavy down
1741	Cinnamon green hen	Large feet
1768	Green cock	Large feet and head
1783	Green hen	Eyebrows
1792	Green cock	Small, narrow head

Remarks Both feed well. Hen removed down from chicks.

A patch applied to a damaged egg.

When the chicks have left the nest you may add other points regarding the excellence or failings of individual birds in your master ledger. These may read *Lovely type, stands well off perch.*
Still later after moulting it may also read *Excellent body colour, mask and spots.*

All records must be accurately kept and checked against the ring number before the birds are released into the aviary. Write everything down and never leave anything to memory. If you are using artificial lighting and have no dimmer or pilot light make sure the hens have returned to the nest before the lights are turned off.   Cleanliness is also very important, keep cages, nest boxes and drinking vessels reasonably clean and always ensure that there is plenty of seed available. Insects, especially red mite, can be easily eliminated with dusting powders or aerosol sprays. Always take care that these sprays are not harmful to birdlife.

An efficient filing system is the key to successful breeding.

Breeding

Because of differences in climate and temperature, preferred breeding times vary throughout the world.

An average nesting cycle lasts about eleven weeks and generally there are two a year, therefore, the overall breeding programme lasts about five months. As budgerigars will generally nest at any time of the year it is necessary to allow them to breed only when the best results will be obtained. Consideration must also be given to the ring issue date if one intends to exhibit the budgerigars in young bird classes. Thus, breeding time in the tropics ranges from April to October but in most other areas breeding time is from June to December. This climatic period, that is from early winter to early summer, is also the preferred breeding time in Europe and most other parts of the world.

Budgerigars are gregarious and will breed more readily if one pair is within sight or sound of another pair. There are two methods practised in the breeding of budgerigars: *controlled breeding* — the method preferred by the exhibitionist, and *colony breeding* — a method practised by fanciers with an outdoor aviary or a large cage.

Controlled breeding is carried out with individual pairs in an aviary or breeding cage of the type described in the chapter, Aviaries, Cages and Appliances. With the aid of carefully kept records this method enables the breeder to select individual pairs to produce offspring with many particular objectives in mind. With correct attention to this method many more youngsters of a much higher quality can be produced.

Colony breeding is carried out in the one cage, where a hen may mate with any number of cocks. As a result, the parentage of the cock and the pedigree of the young are unknown. Another disadvantage of the colony system of breeding is that hens often fight and raid other nests, breaking and throwing out eggs or fatally attacking the youngsters. The advantages are that there is much less work involved in colony breeding and if one is fortunate enough to have a compatible group one may find this method of breeding to be less time consuming.

Controlled breeding

The main moult generally takes place in April, or just prior to the breeding season. This moult places a heavy drain on the bird's system and its physical condition falls well below normal. As a bird be-comes older the oncoming moult becomes increasingly harder to bear physically and they need more time than younger birds to complete it. Many of them fail, thus the term *stuck in the moult*. This means that the budgerigar, after looking run down for some time, has succumbed and died.

After the heavy moult all the birds need a little time to replenish their body with the lost elements so necessary to restore their vitality ready for the oncoming breeding season. This replenishment is only possible if a good feeding programme and an adequate supply of minerals and chemicals are provided. Another point most fanciers who exhibit birds forget is that the birds need plenty of exercise and rest. It should also be noted that over-exhibiting of budgerigars (as many do) will prove fatal to fertility results in the breeding cage.

Better results may be obtained if you fly the cocks and the hens together and then separate them three to four weeks prior to pairing up. Under these conditions the birds are more active: hens, instead of sitting contentedly, are pursued by cocks trying to impress them. Leave a few old infertile cocks with the hens after the separation of cocks and hens because this is helpful in keeping them active and alert.

A budgerigar must be in top breeding condition otherwise you are wasting your own and the bird's time by pairing it up. It is also useless to mate a bird in condition with one that is not. How often one hears the old story, 'They will come into condition in the breeding cage'. They rarely do, and the end results will nearly always be the same: clear or infertile eggs; failure to hatch or young dead in the shell; death on hatching; or failure to feed the young. Usually these faults are blamed on the birds, but in most cases it is the breeder's fault. The birds did not ask to be paired up, that decision is made for them.

When suitable weather conditions occur the budgerigar's breeding cycle condition peaks about every seven weeks and at these times the signs of readiness to breed are observable. They will be constantly and briskly flying about and after landing will seem to flex their wing muscles. The hen will dip her back in readiness for the mating procedure. Cocks will continuously tap the perch with their beak, and their head feathers will rise as they perform a type of crowing act. The birds may chirp and sing continuously, especially at night, even though there may be no moonlight. They will even try to feed and mate with birds of the same sex, although this habit is more obvious in male birds.

Starting with the right conditions – a breeding pair in a roomy breeding cabinet on the correct diet.

Hens will begin chewing at everything in sight and fight over parts of the aviary where they are trying to make a nest. In the eyes of both hens and cocks the white ring of the iris will become larger, causing the pupil to be smaller. This feature, which is often observed when birds are going through the actual mating process, should also be present prior to pairing. It is more pronounced in cock birds.

The cere of the cock will be shiny blue except on Lutinos, Albinos, Fallows, Lacewings and Recessive Pieds; on these it will be purplish-flesh coloured. All hens' ceres will range from light to nut-brown. In addition, all birds will be showing their full complement of feathers which should be tight, especially in large- or buff-feathered birds.

Before any pairing is undertaken make sure the cage is prepared with seed, water and grit. If this is done you will not have to disturb the birds during their settling-in period.

If you feed greenfood do it on a regular basis, the earlier in the day the better because if moisture is still present on the greens the hen will role and flutter in it so that the moisture is distributed over her feathers. This moisture will then be absorbed by the eggs when she returns to her nest, thus preventing the eggs from drying out.

Pairing

The period of fertility in budgerigars varies: some buff-feathered birds may only be fertile for their first breeding season. However, despite the inevitable exceptions to the rule, all birds may produce

well for four years before fertility begins to wane.

I recommend that a bird should be at least nine months old before it is paired and even then the bird would have to have shown very early maturity. Hens left until they are twelve months old will give better results. Ideal partners would be if either one or both have had the experience of a previously successful breeding cycle. If an inexperienced pair is used they may require a little more time to begin mating correctly and to adjust themselves for the natural reproduction cycle ahead.

Some breeders introduce the hen to the breeding cage for a few days prior to the cock so that she can become used to her new surroundings. My preference is to introduce the pair to the breeding cage at the same time. When the nest box should be introduced varies: if the birds are in prime breeding condition I believe the nest box should be available from the start.

Clean sawdust, sieved to remove any long splinters and dust, both of which may produce problems if not removed, should be placed in the nest box. Before laying, the hen will settle herself in by scratching around and removing most of the sawdust from the nest. This activity is instinctive, for example, a wild budgerigar would at times need to do this to rid her nest of unwanted materials.

Regardless of the plan used when a pair of birds has been selected to become partners the best results are generally obtained if they are physically attracted to one another. If a hen begins to act aggressively toward a cock or vice versa, it is advisable to split them up before they cause serious damage to one another. However, if this particular pairing is required the birds may be placed in separate breeding cages with a wire partition between them. Make sure both birds cannot see or have any body contact with birds in the adjoining cages and they may, in time, become more familiar with one another. If the hen has a nest box and you notice her looking for the cock or spending time, especially at night, in the nest, place the cock in her cage first thing in the morning, preferably before the hen has left the nest because at this time of day birds seem to be more virile. If mating does not take place after this has been tried for a number of days you can forget about success this time. If you are determined though, success may be possible later, after the hen has had a complete laying and rearing cycle with another cock.

When you notice the hen staying in the nest for long periods send her from it mornings and evenings to help ensure she mates. This can be done by tapping or knocking the box with your knuckles before checking the nest. The hen will become accustomed to this and when any inspection is to be made she will be prepared for it, and will not scatter and break eggs because of an unexpected intrusion.

If, within three weeks, the hen shows no sign of becoming heavy around the vent or the droppings have not become larger (signs that laying is imminent) you should separate the pair by replacing either the cock or the hen. A hen that has shown all tendencies of laying but has not done so after a week often never will. She may be an internal layer or may even have ruptured, in which case she would be useless in any breeding programme.

Fertilisation

Fertilisation is the first step in any breeding exercise and it used never to be a very difficult process for the small varieties of budgerigar. Once, if after mating the hen relaxed and her wings were seen to go into a brisk shaking down action it was always an indication that she had taken the cock correctly for fertilisation. Now, however, we have bigger birds, with longer and sometimes buff to double-buff feathers. With these more recent varieties it is difficult to know whether mating has been successful.

I will explain the difficulty of proper fertilisation as it was explained to me by a good friend in the United Kingdom, one of the top breeders in the world today. He is not a believer in any cutting or removal of feathers from the vent area as some people are. The feathers are there for softness and

Eggs in various stage of incubation.

to guide and transport the sperm into the hen. He believes that it is not the feathers that are the problem but the underdown, which can sometimes be extra heavy, for example, most cock-headed hens have this type of heavy down. When the mating process is in progress correct copulation may not occur but the sperm may creep along the feathers to complete its journey into the hen. If the underdown is present, however, it will absorb the sperm so that fertilisation cannot take place. Fitness shown in this area is perhaps the sensible key. This will become apparent when one selects a hen with a pronounced vent laying parallel with her body; and a cock whose vent protrudes at right angles to his body. Fertilisation problems with two such birds will rarely occur.

Eggs

Long preparations and a properly planned feeding programme are necessary if the hen is to produce good eggs because the formation of the egg will take some of the calcium that has been stored in parts of the hen's bone structure. The yolk of the egg should be rich in colour if the youngster is to develop into a strong and healthy chick and a supply of greens given to the birds before laying will ensure this, just as it does for poultry eggs. The importance of a balanced diet, which includes greens, is explained in more detail in the chapter, Feeding.

Eggs may vary in both shape and size: spherical or oval, large or small. It is important to remember

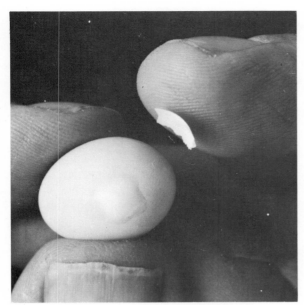

A damaged egg just prior to a patch being applied.

very thin. In both cases air has penetrated the shell because of insufficient shell formation. In extreme cases the hen will lay soft-shelled eggs. These occurrences may be remedied quickly by promptly supplying lime water to the pair.

Infertile eggs
Check your perches for the cause of infertile eggs: that they are neither smooth nor insecure. Alternatively, a perch that is angular can be rounded off in varying degrees. If necessary, two perches can also be placed 50 mm (2 in) apart to allow the hen to balance easier during mating — this is particularly successful with hens that have only one leg.

Punctured eggs
In most cases this is caused by long pointed toe-nails on either the cock or the hen and can be remedied by clipping the nails. Other causes include being frightened from the nest and fighting. An egg outside the nest may have become attached to the feathers and been carried out accidently. Also the hen may have laid while sitting on the perch so that the egg has dropped to the floor, resulting in some indentation in the shell. If the break has not penetrated the inner membrane and allowed the air into the egg it can be saved, no matter what stage of development it is in. If you have another piece of eggshell (I find hatched shells the best because they are more pliable) fashion a piece to cover the break, allowing at least 3 mm (⅛ in) overlap onto the shell. Put a small amount of glue (a P.V.A. wood glue will do) on the area to be covered and on the egg patch. Place the patch on the egg and gently smooth over, wipe off the excess glue. Place the egg back in the nest as soon as the glue has lost its tackiness.

Egg eaters
Either bird can be at fault. I have found the only solution is to make a hole in the centre of the concave in the nest so that the egg will drop through onto soft material where the culprit cannot reach it. This egg then has to be fostered out to another pair.

Outside layers
The hen that continually lays outside the nest and will not sit on replaced eggs or marbles may be induced to lay inside the nest if one constructs a long nest-box and adds a large round tunnel-like entrance (a piece of large bamboo is ideal). Alternatively one may add the round entrance to the existing box. This tunnel will make a nest

that the size of the egg does not determine the size of the chick. Inside the egg there is an inner membrane which surrounds the white and the yolk. Tiny blood veins form the life germ at the top of the yolk and eventually envelope it and the white. The chick absorbs the yolk, which is its food in the shell, through its abdomen. At the blunt end of the egg is the air sac.

Generally a hen lays every second day and the number of eggs laid varies. Thus, although incubation lasts eighteen days and is carried out by the hen only, one should allow twenty days from the first egg laid because the hen does not usually sit until she has laid the second egg. The crucial period in incubation is the first twenty-four hours and during this early stage the egg should be subject to constant temperature.

The fertility of an egg can be tested after six days of incubation by placing it over a light to view the early formation of the blood vessels. Generally it is rare for every egg to hatch and an indication of what is happening inside the shell is often provided by its external appearance. For example, just prior to hatching the shell will change in colour from a pearly whiteness to a grey. Similarly, if the young is dead in the egg the shell will turn a grey-black and have a white-pink tinge in parts.

Clear eggs
These may not have been infertile. On close inspection one may find that some seem to have small bumps, usually at one end; others may be

darker and will give the hen a feeling of security. These birds are not unlike some pairs in the wild who prefer to raise their brood deep inside a long hollow limb.

Egg binding

Egg binding is an inability to dispel the egg. A hen in this condition spends less time in the nest and it is usually obvious that she is in a very distressed condition. When this is suspected check her eggs to see if the due egg has been laid. Other obvious features are that she has a fluffed-out appearance and the vent area has become very heavy. Treatment for this condition is explained in the chapter, Diseases and Ailments.

Cold eggs

It is not impossible to save the eggs of hens that have become sick or have died. Even though the eggs may have been cold for hours the chick will often survive and the eggs can be placed under foster mothers: the only setback is that the eggs take a little extra time to hatch after becoming cold during incubation.

Marking eggs

Marking eggs with their nest number and the sequence number in which the egg was laid is essential when fostering to other pairs. Felt-tipped pens, available in six different colours, are very useful for marking eggs, especially if there are eggs from various pairs in one nest. This practice is particularly important if the eggs are to be returned to the original parents.

It is not so necessary to be particular about marking eggs from one pair if the eggs are being fostered permanently to pairs with infertile eggs or to an obviously different variety. For example, transferring the eggs of Normals to foster parents that are Lutinos. Nevertheless accurate records of egg transfers are important for future reference.

Hatching

When the chick breaks through the membrane into the air sac it is a living creature. It now needs all the strength it has absorbed from the yolk to chip away the egg shell. To do this it will use the temporary egg tooth on the top of the upper beak first to break through the shell, and then to chip around in a complete circle until it is able to free itself by virtually pushing the lid off the egg.

I have noticed that from the first sign of the chipped egg it has sometimes taken the chick two days to release itself from the shell. One is tempted to assist them from the egg but I believe this is unwise. You will lose more than you will ever save as in many cases they will be premature.

The most helpful hint prior to and during hatching is to provide a supply of moisture, especially if the weather conditions are very dry. Every time you open the nest box to inspect the eggs blow your moist breath over them. Likewise, when you see or know eggs are about to hatch you may moisten them with warm water or saliva, or, if your birdroom floor is concrete wet it down, alternatively wet bags may be placed on the floor. A very fine light spray may also be used over the eggs in the nest box.

The only time I would advocate helping a chick from the egg is when there is a lack of moisture. On inspection of the chipped egg you will see that the membrane has dried, perhaps sticking to the chick's head and restricting its movements. Dampen the egg and, with the aid of the quill end of a large feather, proceed carefully to remove the cap from the egg and the dry membrane from the chick. After this has been done and you can see the chick will have no more trouble releasing itself from the rest of the egg return it to the nest. If the chick is nearly exhausted by its ordeal you may feed it a few drops of warm water, with brandy or whiskey added, in an eye dropper to give it the strength it needs to take crop milk from its mother.

As budgerigars seldom reject young from other pairs it is possible to move them from nest to nest, especially in their early stage of development. If young to be fostered are not large enough to ring they can easily be marked with felt markers and here again one can use a different colour for young from different nests. Mark a leg and the top of the head: this may have to be repeated daily as it tends to wear off.

Raising young

Observation of newly hatched young is critical if they are to survive. Eggs are usually laid around mid-day and they tend to hatch during the morning, thus allowing the youngster to be fed with crop milk by the early afternoon. If there is no evidence that the hen has started to feed by nightfall, replace it with a youngster that is three or four days old and foster the newly-hatched youngster with another hen: she may commence to feed the older young as it will be stronger and its beak larger and therefore easier for her to locate. If she will not feed the three- or four-day old either, return it to its original nest. On the hatching of her second egg the hen will usually feed but if not the above procedure may have to be repeated. An alternative method is to feed the young with a little Complan mixed in boiling water. Place the baby on its back and feed it with an eye dropper when the liquid is lukewarm. Even a little water will help the youngster to survive because the most common cause of death at this early stage is dehydration.

Budgerigars feed by regurgitation. After hatching, the cock feeds the hen who in turn feeds the young. She also produces a milk in her crop which is fed to the very young and it is unwise to place too many newly hatched chicks under one hen if she is not capable of keeping up the crop milk. That this is the case is indicated by the presence of seed in the crops of the baby chicks.

The crop milk, a secretion very rich in protein, is essential for the newly hatched offspring. It is their first food and an examination of the crop of youngsters during the first week will reveal a soft creamy substance. Gradually the diet will be supplemented by whole seeds and greenfood and at this time the cock may take over some of the direct feeding. Good parents should have the crops of their youngsters crammed full by nightfall and well-fed chicks will always be quiet and contented. Hungry ones, on the other hand, will be forever calling for food and will quite often fall out of the nest.

As soon as young are starting to hatch you may introduce soaked seed or similar soft food to the parents in the afternoon. If you are using a

Inside the nest, a chick emerges from its egg to join its older nestmates born two and four days before.

A normal cycle of hatching with chicks two to ten days old.

birdroom that is artificially lit you may give it to them later. Any other feeding you think may be beneficial should also be introduced. It is advisable to carry out this extra feeding at the same time every day as the parents will begin to expect it and will not feed correctly until they have received it.

When soaked or soft food is fed you will have to keep an eye on the youngster's beaks, particularly the top one because the horn of the top beak does not become hard until the youngster is about to begin to crack its own seed. In additon, it is common for food to catch under the hooked part of the beak. This food, if not cleaned out daily, will build up, set hard and cause malformation. This build-up can also occur on the lower beak around the tongue and should be removed daily with the hooked end of a nail file or similar device.

Foster parents can be specially paired for the breeding season to help produce more young and if you are faced with rearing problems they will prove invaluable. Pairs whose eggs are infertile can still be used by placing fertile eggs under the hen. Better results will be obtained this way than if one removes their infertile eggs and have them re-lay immediately.

Pairs should be allowed to rear how ever many young they can successfully feed and this will only be determined by observation. Never allow them less than two as the adults will become complacent and bored and brutal habits may develop.

If one parent dies the other will generally continue feeding, but keep an eye on it to ensure the young are being fed properly and if they are not it will be necessary to reduce the load by giving some of them over to the care of foster parents. Sometimes pairs simply become taxed with feeding

A contented hen with two to three week old youngsters.

being squashed and smothered when some hens sit tight. Sitting tight will also cause the youngsters legs to become splayed. The cure for splayed legs is in the chapter, Diseases and Ailments.

Care and cleanliness

The hardening of loose or wet droppings around the birds' feet and claws should be cleaned off regularly to prevent malformations along the toes. Soften the built-up droppings in warm water first to make cleaning easier. Be careful, however, when cleaning around the toes as one can easily remove the nail as well. Where this build-up occurs on the end of the tail feathers the same procedure can be used although care should be taken not to remove the whole feather. Regular cleaning of the nest and the sprinkling of fresh sawdust and a little grit or sand on the floor will help to alleviate this problem.

Feather plucking

This is a very frustrating problem because instead of a nest of chicks that are nearly feathered, one suddenly finds, the next time one looks, that the chicks are red raw and most probably minus their wing and rump feathers as well. In extreme cases the feathers, skin and scalps may also have been removed and if the young are not dead they will need to be destroyed. As a rule, if a hen starts to pluck she will never stop. Sometimes it is the cock who is the culprit so be wary of both unless there is obvious proof, such as blood on either of their beaks.

Some birds never go further than to remove down from chicks. This is only parental fussing. Nevertheless, if ever you hear birds squawking in the nest, it is wise to investigate immediately. If the hen is the culprit remove her and leave the cock to finish rearing them.

Although there is nothing that can be done about the determined plucker one method that is successful for helping to alleviate feather plucking is to supply the pair with suet (or similar). Oil sprays are also available. It is not known why these work.

Features to observe in the nest

The more observant you become the more you will learn. Sometimes a bird with exceptionally good qualities can be seen at an early stage. Those qualities which should be noted down in your records at this time may include the appearance of such features as: heavy down after the first few days; and eyebrows and collar of down showing out against the feathers around the neck. In the United

Chicks at four weeks, and nearing the final stages of the development of their feathers.

their young and these can be given a tonic such as Hepasol. Also, tempting them with some other types of seeds and greens may rejuvenate them for the job ahead.

Cold young

When hens die and the young appear cold and lifeless place them in your cupped hands and blow your warm breath on them. If they stir place them under a foster mother. Alternatively, they can be revived by placing them where light passes through glass.

Sitting tight

Always leave two or three infertile (clear) eggs with the hen after the young have hatched, at least until they are five days old. This will prevent them from

A pair commencing to rear their second brood.

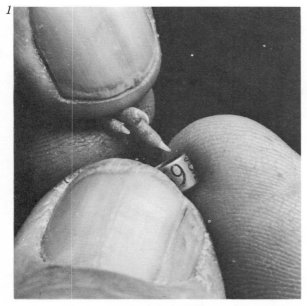

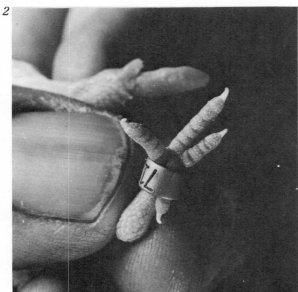

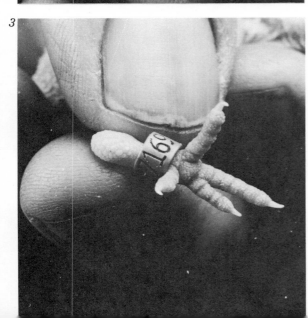

Kingdom this latter feature is carried by some of the best exhibition birds.

In Australia, if the mask is bright yellow it generally indicates either a yellow-face or a bird that is carrying the violet factor. In the United Kingdom, on the other hand, this yellow face is a normal feature in Greens, which also carry their nest cap much higher on the head than those in Australia. A Clearwing carrying its wing colouring in a bar effect across its chest or on its rump will end up maturing with a wing that is free of markings.

A bird with a good head can be recognised with ease at a very early age, even at birth. The eye colour should also be noted. This may help determine the pedigree at maturity, for example, the eye of a Cinnamon is pink only for the first five days.

Pieds can also be recognised early by the variation of skin colouring.

Ringing young

A bird that is five to ten days old should be big enough to ring. First ensure its legs and toes are clean, then to ring the bird, hold it gently in the hand with the head downwards and the feet up; hold the three front toes together and press the back toe close to the leg. Slip the ring onto the leg using a large quill feather to ease the back toe down through the ring. If any difficulty is experienced a little Vaseline on the toes will help to ease the ring on gently.

Leaving the nest

Youngsters generally leave the nest voluntarily at the age of five weeks. They should be able to crack seed by themselves before they are removed from the breeding cage. When placing them in the training cage ensure that plenty of seed is scattered on the floor.

Many problems are avoided if youngsters are swapped around so that each nest contains youngsters that are all about the same stage of development. This can be carried out from just after the ringing. The advantages of this method is that large nests of youngsters are all ready to leave the nest at the same time. This alleviates the problem of late hatching youngsters who have been left far behind in their development because they have been forced from the nest prematurely.

French Moult

If youngsters start losing wing and tail feathers and

The three steps necessary to place a closed ring on a chick. Take care when easing the back toe down through the ring to complete step three.

in extreme cases body feathers, they have French Moult. This condition is explained more fully in the Chapter, Diseases and Ailments.

Second round

If the hen begins to lay again when young are still in the nest box save the new eggs from being broken or chipped by fostering them out. Replace them with clear eggs and the hen will begin to sit again; then when the young have left the breeding cage return her eggs to her and remove the clear eggs.

Often a hen that has started to re-lay may become a little aggressive towards the young still in the nest, thus making the removal of the chicks necessary. Young that are fully feathered and have half-grown tail feathers are quite capable of standing and gripping the perch although they may huddle in a corner at night so you can place some sawdust there for them to settle into. As long as they have feed in their crops they will be alright. If they have empty crops in the evening you will have to return them to the nest for the hen to feed and remove them next morning. Repeat this procedure until they are feeding themselves. Any young that are not being fed by their parents will have to be fostered out. If, for any reason, a youngster is not feeding itself when taken from its parents and you have tried unsuccessfully to get other adult birds to feed it, you may give it a drink of glucose water with an eye dropper before placing it in a cage with its nest mates; often one of these birds will begin to feed it.

If a pair has produced the type of youngsters required in the first round and the hen has laid ten

fertile eggs in the second round and you wish to hatch them all, place the first four eggs under a foster parent and allow the hen to sit on the remainder. Good feeders can easily handle six young on the second round because the days are generally much longer, thus allowing them more time to feed.

Should a hen be showing signs of re-laying and you want to break up the pair to stop them from breeding again, take her from the breeding cage and place her in another cage. This will enable you to keep an eye on her in case she shows signs of egg binding. This precaution also allows her eggs to dry up and gives her a chance to recuperate before being let out into the aviary. Check the cock bird, too, to see if he is continuing to feed the young. If he is not you will have to return the hen and remove the nest box if the young are big enough.

If you require a third round of young from a pair let the hen re-lay and repeat the procedure suggested for the second nest, but foster out all the eggs this time. Do not let her feed a third round if she has already raised two nests because it may overtax the pairs system and be a complete waste of time. Before returning parent birds to the aviary after feeding is finished allow them a few days rest.

Increasing the offspring from one bird

Mating of budgerigars to more than one partner in a breeding season is quite easily accomplished. As this system is used to produce more young than usual from a certain bird you will have to have foster pairs in use to get the results you are after. It is wise, however, to let these birds have the first round of youngsters in a natural cycle or problems

A typical colony breeding nest arrangement.

with the birds may occur later on, for example, failure to sit or punctured eggs.

One should also avoid the canary breeding system of running two or three hens with the one cock at the same time. A sound programme for a cock that has reared his first round is to leave him with the hen until she has finished laying her second clutch of eggs. Then fly him in the aviary for a few days to revitalise him before pairing him with another hen.

A hen is a little more difficult. You can remove her, prior to re-laying, to another breeding cage or allow her to re-lay and remove the cock before she has stopped laying. Foster her eggs and remove the nest box. After a few days introduce a new cock to the hen and if they are compatible the nest box can be replaced.

The only problem when re-using hens is that they may still be fertile to the previous cock. To overcome this they are better paired to a cock of a different colour or variety, that is, one that will produce different results. For example, if the hen is Cinnamon and the first cock is Cinnamon, all their young will be Cinnamon. Pair the Cinnamon hen to a Normal cock and the progeny must be Normals.

Quick round

If a pair's eggs are infertile, replace two of them with fertile eggs. After the eggs have hatched and the youngest is four days old, replace it with a ten days old chick. Then, the next day, if both are fed replace the smallest with one two weeks old. You may try larger ones again after a few days. The result is that one ends up with three youngsters of the same size in the nest. By using this method one can reduce the breeding cycle by at least two weeks. Thus, when a hen re-lays, there is a better chance that the eggs will be fertile and that she will lay more eggs.

Incubators

Anybody that has had a long association with the breeding of birds will agree that, although the budgerigar is one of the easiest birds to breed, there is never any short cut to success. For this reason, I personally cannot see any advantage in using an incubator and I believe that its use would only indicate the inability of the user to handle the ordinary problems that arise during this period.

Colony breeding

The colony system of breeding was the first method used in the breeding of budgerigars in captivity. It was carried out first in Europe and its large-scale success has been responsible for making the budgerigar the most popular cage bird in the world.

The wild budgerigar breeds as nature dictates, by the supply of necessary seeds and herbs. We in turn have to restrict their breeding in the aviary because there they have a plentiful supply of seed at all times and are therefore capable of breeding all the year round. Control is exercised by the removal of the nest boxes, preferably at times of extreme hot or cold weather, although even when nests are provided and the colony is contented a hen still may choose to nest under a piece of wood or similar material on the ground. Alternatively, she may settle herself in a little nook or corner on the floor to raise her brood. This behaviour is more likely, however, when there is the urge to breed and nest boxes are not available.

In colony breeding it is advisable to allow two nest boxes for each pair and these should be all placed at the same height in the aviary to help avoid hens fighting for a particular nest. Nests used should be of the same design and the entrance hole should be on the side furthest from the concave so the hen may be more secluded. The attachment of a funnel entrance to the nest may help to discourage birds from disturbing and fighting one another — hens are notorious fighters during breeding and often a troublesome hen in a colony will enter nests of other breeding pairs, fighting the hens and breaking the eggs or, after forcing the mother from the nest will kill or maim any youngsters in the nest. It is advisable to dispense with any such troublesome hens.

It is possible to have odd cocks in a colony system but never odd hens. Also the fewer the pairs in a colony system the better the results. As a rule, pairs do seem to feed their young better in an aviary and fertility is better. Often, too, a pair that will not breed in a breeding cage will often breed without any problems after being placed in an aviary on their own or with other pairs. In addition, the youngsters leave the nest sooner in an aviary and there are less problems with hens not feeding and feather plucking, probably because it is a more natural environment and there is more freedom of flight.

As with controlled breeding, best results are obtained if only two successive nests of youngsters are allowed. To bring breeding to a halt and give the birds the rest they need one has simply to remove their nest boxes.

A wide selection of hens at a commercial aviary.

8 BUYING A BUDGERIGAR FOR BREEDING

Much of the relevant information for purchasing budgerigars is contained in other chapters; for instance, the Chapter, The Budgerigar as a Pet, has a section devoted to the buying of birds suitable for pets and talkers. And, in other chapters there is more detailed advice on how to improve specific features in breeding.

The majority of budgerigar fanciers begin in a humble way and many have extremely poor results initially. Hopefully, therefore, the principles I shall describe will bring good results and provide a sound basis for the development of a successful hobby.

When buying stock it is wise not to act in haste. Patience is a virtue, regardless of whether one is buying one or many birds. For most beginners, the biggest stumbling block will be that of having little or no idea of what one is looking for or at. It is wise, therefore, either to seek advice from someone who is experienced or to read the relevant chapters in this book in order to prepare you for your purchases and clarify your objective. Only then can one set about the task of the purchasing a bird with any degree of confidence.

If one merely desires to keep these attractive birds for the pleasure of watching their antics then it will not be necessary to evenly match the number of sexes. In fact, a group of cock birds on their own are quite compatible and create a very pleasing spectacle. If, however, some hens are introduced to the cage or aviary, then it would be preferable to have as many hens as cock birds.

When you intend to commence breeding with budgerigars you will, of course, have to purchase a true breeding pair, that is, a cock and hen. In addition, one would do well to remember that in nature budgerigars gather together in flocks to breed and one pair on their own, out of sight or sound of any other budgerigars, may not commence to breed. Thus, it may be necessary to purchase two breeding pairs.

When buying birds one is, in the main, in the hands of the seller and it is in these people you will have to place your trust. Unfortunately, some of these sellers, whether they be dealers or breeders, will often make transactions that later prove to be somewhat different than your intended purchase. This may be an honest mistake caused by a lack of knowledge and the seller may be only too willing to rectify his or her error. In the main, however, you can only be guided in these matters by the notices usually displayed by the seller.

Nevertheless, there are some important points that one does have control over and which should be taken into consideration. Firstly, the health of the bird is critical, especially if one is introducing new stock to healthy stock. When contemplating a purchase from a dealer or any business catering for the pet trade, it is wise to make a sound assessment of the condition of all the animals and different types of birds, regardless of how small or large the place is. If they all look healthy and the establishment is clean you can be reasonably assured that the business is run satisfactorily. The same stringent test should be applied to a private breeder.

Secondly, do not expect a healthy bird, used to a clean environment, to survive in new, unhealthy surroundings. Even though your birds may thrive under such conditions, any new arrival will have to develop an immunity over a period of time and to adapt to the new conditions. For these reasons, therefore, it may not be the fault of the person who has sold the bird if it sickens and dies.

A further mistake is to release the newly purchased bird into an aviary in the late afternoon. This means that the newcomer has no time to accustom itself to its new surroundings before nightfall and it will, when disturbed, invariably fly blindly into unknown objects and injure itself, sometimes fatally.

A healthy bird moves vigorously from place to place. If it is caged on its own it should call out to other budgerigars within sight or sound. The eyes are bright and alert and when the bird is handled it should always feel solid in the grasp of your hand. Prior to, or at this point, an inspection should be made of the vent area for stained feathers. These stains can indicate that a bird is suffering from diarrhoea or some other sickness. Although these symptoms may be temporary, it is wise to avoid the purchase of these birds.

When a bird is being purchased for breeding, check also that there is no enlarged, spongy area in front of, or surrounding the vent. If there is any evidence of this (more obvious in hens) the cause could be a tumor or a rupture, in which case the bird is useless for breeding purposes. Other signs of poor health are when the eye appears almond-shaped and dull in colour. In addition, sticky facial feathers, held together by a white mucous, which in advanced cases will be in the form of an encrustation, will certainly mean the bird is not well. Signs of a dull white film on the cere are a further indication of a bird that is not physically fit, especially if it is during the bird's moulting period.

Some birds moult after they have been purchased. This is no cause for alarm because moulting is a natural process brought about at times by a change in the bird's environment. It is a temporary condition only.

Age

Once a budgerigar has acquired its adult plumage, that is, at four to six months of age, there is little hope of determining its correct age. For this reason a leg ring should be placed on the leg when the bird is one week old. A closed aluminium leg ring should have the year of birth, plus other symbols and numbers engraved into it. This enables one to determine the bird's age to the nearest year. Make sure the ring on the bird you intend to purchase has not been cut, otherwise you have no guarantee of its real age.

When you require breeding hens it is best to give preference to birds that are no older than one or two years of age because the older the hen, the less offspring it will produce. Generally, cock birds retain their vigour for breeding for a greater number of years than a hen.

Often you will see large good quality birds for sale. Sometimes these birds will be wearing a closed ring and have noticeably large chests. The latter is a sign of advanced age and inspection of the year engraved on the ring will confirm this. Many of these birds, found at bird-dealers or pet shops have been purchased in a consignment of breeder's surplus stock and although they may still be useful for breeding, others may have been discarded by their previous owners because of troubles or vices

they had during breeding. These may include: failure to lay; infertility; failure to feed young; feather plucking of young; and maiming youngsters.

These are the worst vices one is likely to encounter, but as the seller, like yourself, has purchased these birds on visual appearances only, he or she will have no idea of any of the bird's failings either. And, if the bird shows any failings or habits, it is impossible to know whether or not it has commenced some of them since your purchase, thus making it difficult to apportion blame.

Often, after buying a true pair for breeding, the unknowing purchaser will arrive home with the cherished pair and find out, to his or her eventual dismay, that they are a pair of cock birds. It is rare to end up with a pair of hens as these are the hardest to acquire in adult birds, especially at breeding times. To avoid either situation one should familiarise oneself with cere colours: these are blue in cock birds with the exception of Lutinos, Albinos, Lacewings, Recessive Pieds and Fallows (purplish-flesh colour). A hen's cere is always light to nut-brown and when it is in prime breeding condition the surface will have a rough texture.

This bird with an advanced rupture is useless for breeding.

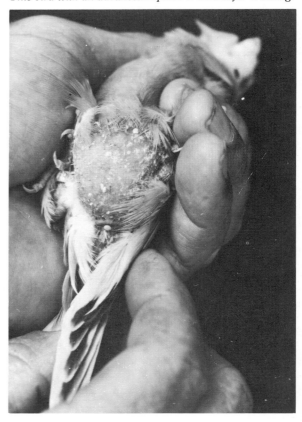

Acquiring an awareness of the many pitfalls involved when buying birds in order to maintain a balance of certain varieties and colours is never easy. This is especially true when breeding on the colony system. Although one may produce other forms when commencing with a pair of a certain variety or colour, it is usual for them to reproduce at least some of their own kind. More information on this subject is found in the chapter, The Laws of Inheritance.

If a continuation of a particular variety or colour is desired, I would recommend the purchase of true breeding pairs, especially when any form of uncontrolled breeding, such as colony breeding, is in use. To ensure that these birds will be continually reproduced, it would be advisable to maintain the number of such birds at half of the total. The following are some examples that may help you to maintain the variety or colour preferred.

1 If one begins with a colony that is composed of a larger percentage of Greens, the result over a period of time would be an aviary of Greens because green is the dominant colour.
2 On the other hand, if Blue birds are wanted one should never introduce a Green, a Yellow, a Lutino, or even a Yellow-face (type 2) because once again, it would be quite possible to finish up with an aviary of Greens.
3 When Lutinos are desired, have only Lutinos, although it is quite possible to breed an odd Albino from these. If you discard the Albinos as they appear, you will get Lutinos only.
4 Albinos, of course, are easy to breed because if Albinos are purchased and kept together no other colour can be produced.
5 Dominant Pieds can only be continually bred while you have a Domonant Pied bird present. Recessive Pieds are a little different as this factor can be hidden and appear although an actual Recessive Pied does not seem to be present. If you have purchased and kept only Recessive Pieds you will always have an aviary of Recessive Pieds.

The following is a comprehensive list of cocks and hens that should never be bought in the belief that they are split for a dominant character because these dominant characters are always visual.

1 Birds split for the variety of Australian or Dutch Dominant Pied.
2 Birds split for the colour of the Australian Grey or Grey-green.
3 A bird split for the colour of Violet.
4 A bird split for the variety of Spangle.
5 Black-eyed Yellows or Whites split for a Grey-wing.
6 A Blue bird split for a Yellow-face.

The laws of inheritance show that it is not possible to breed such birds. Furthermore, one should also avoid the purchase of the following hens for breeding:

1 A hen split for a Lutino or Albino.
2 A hen split for an Opaline.
3 A hen split for a Lacewing or Cinnamon.

These hens cannot be split for any of these characters because they are sex-linked and cannot be carried hidden by a hen. Cock birds, however, can be split for any of these characters. Thus, in order to reproduce any of the above sex-linked varieties it would be advisable to purchase a breeding pair. If a pair is unavailable purchase a cock because, in the majority of cases, all the hens produced will be of the same variety.

A good policy for any beginner, when purchasing birds from a breeder who appears to have stock that is consistently good, is to always purchase a breeding pair. Not only will these birds be more compatible but their offspring should bear a likeness to their parents.

Prices of birds vary and in most countries are very reasonable. As a general rule you will only get what you pay for. Mediocre birds are always cheap: better quality exhibition birds often claim higher prices. New mutations generally command a high price but if they are prolific breeders the price soon falls as all market prices are controlled eventually by the system of supply and demand. The deciding factor will always be how much money you are prepared to pay.

Overall, the buying of birds for breeding is fascinating, especially when you are seeking something special. Most sellers are prepared to give helpful advice but on occasion your awareness and knowledge will prove to be greater. In these cases then, you have the advantage of purchasing a bird that otherwise may have been discarded. The people you meet and the miles of searching for that elusive bird will all add to your store of practical knowledge and a feeling of satisfaction will be your reward when you eventually buy the bird you have been seeking.

9 PREPARATION FOR SUCCESSFUL EXHIBITING

Exhibition points of excellence should only be considered in the light of the structural and feather changes that have been made to take place in the budgerigar. Since the budgerigar was first bred in captivity there has been, as well as selective breeding, the appearance of mutations which have resulted in changes in its structure and outward appearance. These changes are more obvious in outstanding show specimens bred from English stock

The Longflight is an example of the extent of the changes that have been brought about. The breeding of this larger bird has been a result of mutation and careful selection. Some parts of the body have been increased out of proportion to the overall size increase, while other parts have remained the same comparative size. In addition, body feathers are longer and the birds have more underdown, thus causing it to look even larger. The structure and feathering of the head have also undergone obvious changes. This facial feathering is a result of the propagation of another very aptly named mutation, the Pussy-face. The result — a very admirable specimen.

Because the birds must retain their agility and still be capable of good flight and reproduction the changes must be within the bounds of nature. A most interesting point here is that we are able to observe, like Charles Darwin did with the birdlife on the Galapagos Islands, how nature evolves changes which enable a species to adapt to the prevailing conditions. People breeding birds for exhibition and for their own satisfaction achieve similar results by selective breeding, utilising mutations that may have been eliminated in nature.

Training and preparation

The preparation for the exhibiting of budgerigars is by no means a simple matter if one wishes to become very successful. It is very time consuming

Training budgerigars is not difficult, and it is an important part of successful exhibiting. This group has certainly made the judge's task much easier.

and involves a lot of hard work. On the other hand, if one wishes to show birds simply for the fun of it the preparations can be nil. It must be remembered, however, that there are always more losers than winners so you will have to learn to take the rough with the smooth.

The art of showmanship is important and at all times one must have one's ear to the ground in order to pick up some of those finer points which one day may tip the balance on a win or loss. Birds that are being prepared for showing must be approaching top physical condition and if, on the day of judging one has such a bird, with a full complement of feathers laying smooth and close to its body with a nice sheen, one should feel justifiably proud. On the other hand showing birds that are out of condition only makes them worse.

Training birds for showing really begins in the nest box when they are a few days old. Handle them regularly and when feathers begin to appear remove the chicks from the nest box and stroke them. They will soon become quiet and placid. Then, when they are ready to leave the nest and are capable of feeding themselves follow this up by placing them in a training cage. It is advisable not to take them straight from the nest to the aviary as in most cases they will become very hard to train.

An ideal training cage size would be 1.2 m (4 ft) long, 300 mm (12 in) wide and 406 mm (16 in) in height. Should the depth be greater than 300 mm (12 in) it is advisable to have divisional sliders for lessening the width when training is in progress. Perches of various diameters should be placed at least 200 mm (7 in) apart and, if possible placed at least 50 mm (2 in) away from the cage front. To do this, insert a screw into the perch from the back of the cage. This helps prevent the birds from acquiring bad habits like turning somersaults on the perch with the help of the cage front. An old show cage, which is fitted with a slide door, can be attached to the outside of the cage. This allows them to get accustomed to the show cage and also provides a way of removing youngsters if this is necessary. Greens placed in the show cage will entice the birds into it and soon they will be sitting in their of their own accord. Greens can also be used for quietening the birds in the training cage. For example, you should soon be able to place your hands amongst the birds when they are feeding on the greens without them taking any notice of you.

Constant training may be necessary to develop steadiness in this budgerigar.

The bird pictured is displaying overlapping flights and may never be cured of this fault.

Begin working the birds by moving your hands about in front of them and by making them stand correctly and move from perch to perch according to your hand movements. Later you may introduce a judge's stick to lift their wings, touch them on the legs and head, and reverse them on the perch. This is what they will probably encounter later on in their showing experience. The first time they may be shown is at evening club shows or occasionally at day shows especially promoted for unbroken caps or nest feathers (terms used for budgerigars at this stage of development.)

After a period of about two weeks in a trainer the youngsters should be ready to go to the flights. Release them a few at a time to enable them to feel their wings and flight direction without flying into one another. The best time to release them is earlier in the day because this enables them to familiarise themselves with their surroundings.

It is advisable that the birds do not have any further training until they are nearing the completion of their first moult, at which time they will attain their adult plumage. Then, any promising looking youngsters can be caught and placed in pairs in the show cages. This tends to steady them and they soon relax and exhibit their outline. Do not leave them in the show cage too long, a little and often is best. When they are reaching their full feather stage and looking physically fit they may be left in for two hours a day. At first I would place the bird in the show cage with an old stager of the same sex, working them occasionally with hands or stick. When the youngster is steady enough, place it on its own, gradually increasing the length of time. Needless to say, in all of this training the birds should be able to see other birds just as they would under show conditions.

There are some methods which may be useful if a particular bird will not show itself: one is to fill the bottom of the cage with water or turn the cage upside down to make it stand on the perches. Sometimes twirling the cage to and fro to make the bird giddy has a settling down effect. If a bird is really wild one may have to spray it with water until it is soaked and unable to fly. This can be carried out in an old show cage and may have to be repeated many times. While wet the bird may be helped on to the perch with a judge's stick and in time it may stand and gain its confidence. This procedure should only be resorted to if the bird can be completely dry before dark. Still, it must be remembered that good showers are born, not made.

When you have selected your show team check them for broken flight and tail feathers. Pull the broken feathers out firmly in a straight line. Generally flight feathers take four to six weeks to grow, long tail feathers six to eight weeks and spot feathers three to four weeks to reappear. In all cases these times are for naturally moulted feathers. I must stress a warning here: on occasions, feathers which have been forcibly removed will not regrow.

Washing and spraying preparations should commence two or three weeks prior to the show. Any blood stained feathers can be cleaned by washing with soap under running cold water. If blood is left on the feathers it tends to rot them so it is best removed as soon as it is noticed. If you have any birds that are very dirty you will have to wash them. This may be done using a shaving brush and warm water to which is added a little shampoo. After washing place the bird in a warm spot to dry. From now on cleanliness is essential. Remember, the less you have to handle the birds from now on the better — clammy hands tend to take the bloom off the feathers. Spraying of your birds can be undertaken in your aviary, however, if one has placed the budgerigars in a cabinet during the pre-show period as most breeders do it will be necessary to first run them singly into a clean show cage or, better still, a wire cage. Commence with a very light or fine spray of antiseptic diluted in water — 1 teaspoon of antiseptic to 4-5 L (1 gal) of water. Not only will the antiseptic assist in cleansing but it will help deter beak mite as well. Gradually increase the volume of spray until the birds look half-drowned. The regularity of the spraying varies according to the climate. In warm climates daily sprays are best as they seem to hold them in feather. In cooler climates it may be less. Spraying should be reduced three days before the show, so that for the last two days they receive only a very fine spray with pure water. After the spraying place the birds in a warm spot to dry, in front of a heater.

If you have an overspotted bird remove the excess spots five days prior to the show. To avoid removing the wrong feathers push the unwanted spots upwards so that the required spots are still in their place; remove the spot feathers with tweezers or fingernails. Also at this time you may lightly rub glycerine on the beak to give it a nice glossy appearance. This also helps the mask and face feathers to settle down in the final spraying stages. To promote a better sheen on the feathers you may add two teaspoons of glycerine and 1 teaspoon of borax to .57L (1 pint) of water.

Any pin feathers on the head can be stroked down in the direction of the feather growth using a soft cloth or brush dipped in water. This method can also be used to open up newly grown and unopened throat spot feathers because it aids the removal of the wax casing on the feather. Cracked or damaged flight or tail feathers can be repaired by dipping the feathers into boiling water making sure the water does not come into contact with the skin. The excess water can then be wiped off with a soft cloth in the direction of the feather growth. Because the feathers dry quickly this can be done just prior to putting the bird into the show cage ready for dispatch to the show. A word of caution: never place your stickers on the show cage before placing the birds inside. That way there will be no chance of having either the wrong birds in the wrong cages or the wrong class.

The show cage must be clean and nicely painted. Do not paint it the day before the show as not only is the smell overpowering but in many parts the paint may take up to a week to dry. In most cases in Australia seed is placed on the floor of the show cage, this must be clean and free from dust and dirt. If self-coloured, especially Whites, are to be shown you may want to wash the seed and dry it. Never put water in your drinkers until after the bird is judged. Make sure perches and cage fronts are secure, if acceptable pin or tape the door closed.

A guide for beginners

In order to learn the rules and whatever else is required to participate in the exhibiting of

Satisfaction is winning awards in bird shows large and small. This pleased exhibitor has plenty to smile about, after winning awards at the Budgerigar Society Club Show held in Leicester in the U.K.

budgerigars one should first become a member of a specialist budgerigar or mixed-bird society in your area. Most budgerigar shows have different categories within their schedules, mainly open or champion, intermediate, beginner or novice and, at times, junior. Your club will advise you on the category in which your birds are eligible to be shown. Later, if you are successful, they will determine when you will have to step up the ladder. This usually occurs after a specified number of wins, or a period of time laid down in their show rules.

In young or breeder's classes any bird exhibited must be wearing a current year's or season's closed ring. The bird must also have been bred by the exhibitor, whose ring must be registered and issued by a recognised society. Any purchased bird wearing a current year's or season's ring must be exhibited with others in the adult or old bird classes provided.

A good apprenticeship in which to become aware of what is required for a good exhibition bird plus the classes individual birds should be shown in, is to become involved with the stewarding at your club. Part of this job at times entails bringing and returning the classes of birds from the staging to where the judge desires to officiate. Most judges will indicate good and bad points during the judging procedure so one can see the condition your birds should be in if they are to compete for top awards.

If, at any time, a decision is made against a bird you have shown and you are unable to understand the judge's reasoning, seek out the judge at the event and not a week later. He will be only too happy to inform you why that decision was made. Advice may also be sought when you have won an event as your bird may possess a quality you are unaware of.

10 STANDARD OF PERFECTION AND JUDGING

The first Australian standard of perfection I saw was published in 1936. The illustration of this first ideal budgerigar was drawn by Neville Cayley, the celebrated artist and author. It was accompanied by the first body colour chart which consisted of eighteen colours and shades as well as the correct shade of grey for the Greywing, a standard to which we still aim today. An enduring thought on the cover of that edition was, 'Type makes the bird, colouration the variety'.

As standards vary and are being continually upgraded from State to State and country to country there is little chance of outlining a single correct standard of perfection. In each area the standard varies and you will have to purchase your standard of perfection from your ruling body. Unfortunately, because this standard of perfection is not three-dimensional, there are varying interpretations of what should be the Ideal bird. As a result of this inadequacy of the drawings some breeders have made their own three-dimensional version of what an Ideal bird should be. For example, Mr Rodney Harris, who lives in Cornwall, England, has carved from wood two models of perfection, a cock and a hen. His efforts were the culmination of many years work as a champion budgerigar breeder and he has hand-painted them in minute detail, even gluing actual feathers on the mask to cover the beak area where required. On his models the feathers on the chest protrude onto the wing near the shoulder as is seen normally on live birds — a detail not usually present in any drawing of an ideal budgerigar.

It is extremely difficult to describe in words what is required for perfection in an exhibition budgerigar, and even if you could, it would be almost impossible to breed such a specimen. Perfection in the exhibition budgerigar is often only in the eyes of the owner-breeder. Nevertheless, the following comments and explanations may help breeders and exhibitors to gain a better appreciation of some of the qualities desired in an exhibition budgerigar.

Comparisons of any original and present Ideal will see this dramatic change in outline.

Desirable qualities in an exhibition budgerigar

Condition
A bird must be in good health. Birds that are fat, underweight or out of condition for any reason should never be shown.

Balance
The basis for a good outline commences at the head when a bird is standing on the perch at an angle of thirty degrees from the vertical or at eleven or one o'clock. From this point every detail should be studied closely to determine if the remainder of the bird has a pleasing appearance and matches your ideal of perfection.

Type

Most fanciers will agree that there are now two distinct types of exhibition budgerigar. The first is the cock with a very forward and high frontal rise which causes it to appear narrower in the head when viewed from the front. This type of bird is also generally slimmer and therefore tends to look longer. It shows more clearance between the perch and its body and has the ability to make you imagine that it has a vice grip on the perch and is straining to enhance its appearance. The hen of this variety is often referred to as being *cock-headed*. The head may be a little flatter and broader and its body a little wider but it possesses all the other characteristics of the cock of this type.

The second type of cock is often referred to as a *cobbier bird* and has a much wider and flatter head. The beak of this cock is much less visible because of extra feather cover and the extra face width gives it a larger mask area. As a result it appears to have heavy eyebrows. The neck is wide and full, its body thicker, and its chest possibly a little more pronounced. This bird may not have the clearance between the body and the perch that its counterpart has and because of the boldness of the head and neck it may look a little unbalanced. The legs are strong and wide apart with less rump covered by the wings because of the extra body width. The hen of this type has a flatter head and possesses all the qualities of the cock.

Both types are pleasing to the eye and their overall appearance on the day will determine which is judged to be the superior bird.

Head

The crucial point here is the correct positioning of the eye, which should also be bold and bright. Most drawn Ideals have the eye shown in a central position in the head. This placement is incorrect and observation of any bird with a good head shows that the eye is much closer to the beak. The top of the cere and the centre of the eye should appear level and continuation of this level line through to the back of the head should bring us to the base of the outline of the head and the commencement of the line of the back. The beak should be smooth and set well back into a long face.

Mask and spots

The ornamental cheek patch should be much wider than is shown in most ideals. It should also be

Winner of the intermediate section at a Budgerigar Society Club Show.

triangular. On a big spotted bird the cheek patch should half cover the first spot. As well as this the bird should feature six nicely rounded and evenly spaced throat spots on a deep, wide mask.

Cap

The cap should create a nice browy appearance over the eyes when viewed from any angle, but it should not be exaggerated.

Neck

A perfect head can be spoilt by a faulty neck. If it is too long, too short or if it cuts in at the front or is nipped in the back it will make the head appear separate to the body. A good neck is unobtrusive — where the head and body are virtually one.

Best in show at a Budgerigar Society Club Show, Leicester, U.K.

Length and size

Most Ideals are a uniform 215 mm (8½ in) from the crown of the head to the tip of the tail. The length of the bird should be balanced by its size; usually it is left to the judge's discretion to determine if the bird is too big or too small.

Tail

The tail is just as important as the head and should be neatly packed from the butt. The two main tail feathers should blend together and taper slightly toward the tip. They should not have a dropped or raised appearance but should be seen as a continuation of the straight backline. A tail should not be so long as to give the bird a drawn-out appearance, nor should it be too short. It should give the bird a balanced appearance.

Wings

Good wings should be compact and neatly folded and look as if they are part of the body. The ends of the primary flights should just meet over the centre of the tail. The ideal length cannot be measured but there should be body colour showing on the tail, below the wing tips. Wing faults are many, dropped wings (sometimes only one) are common, as are crossed or scissored wings. Birds with heavy secondary flights are not uncommon but long-flighted birds are becoming less prominent. We rarely see short-flighted birds.

Legs and feet

Legs should not be stick-like but should be straight and strong. The feet and claws should be big-boned to enable the bird to support the weight of its body on and off the perch.

The best Pied exhibited at a Budgerigar Society Club Show.

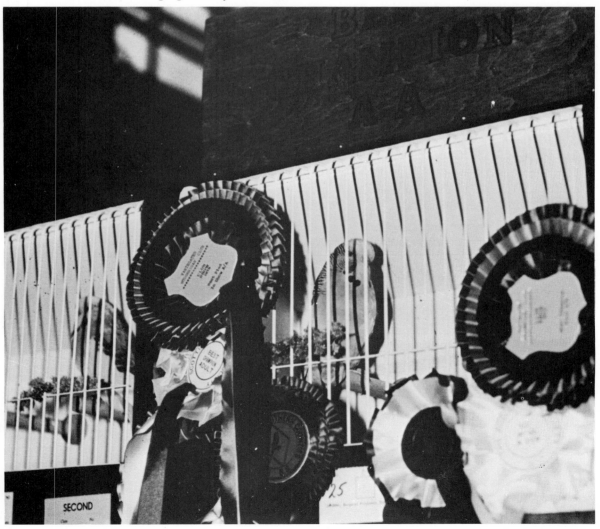

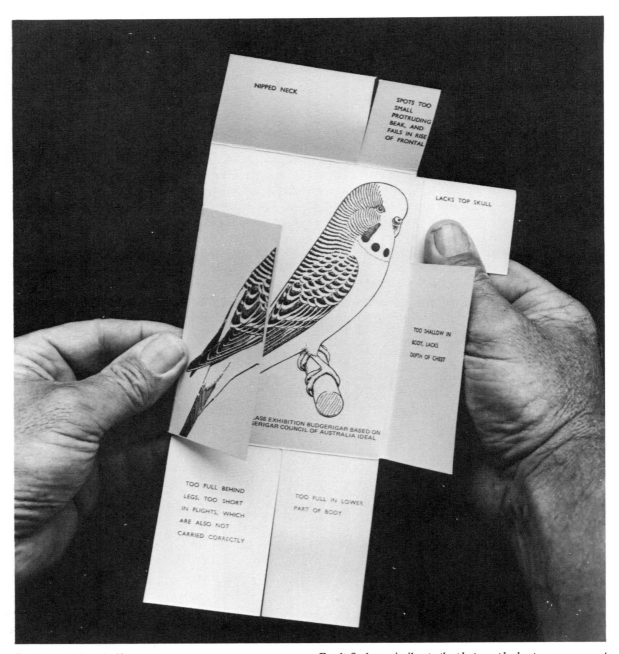

Labels on the fault finder card:

NIPPED NECK

SPOTS TOO SMALL PROTRUDING BEAK, AND FAILS IN RISE OF FRONTAL

LACKS TOP SKULL

TOO SHALLOW IN BODY, LACKS DEPTH OF CHEST

...ASS EXHIBITION BUDGERIGAR BASED ON ...GERIGAR COUNCIL OF AUSTRALIA IDEAL

TOO FULL BEHIND LEGS, TOO SHORT IN FLIGHTS, WHICH ARE ALSO NOT CARRIED CORRECTLY

TOO FULL IN LOWER PART OF BODY

Fault finders, similar to the photographed copy, are an asset for the beginner so as to distinguish a bird's failings.

Body and back lines

The body should be nicely rounded, that is, across the bird rather than along it. All hollows, especially a nipped neck and chestiness, which are mainly visible on hens, destroy clean-cut body lines. The body curvature should commence at the mask and end at the lower tail coverts. One common fault is that the curve is interrupted between the legs and the tail, giving the bird a cut-off appearance. The backline should appear as a straight line from the top of the nape to the tip of the tail and show no hollows or lumps.

Colour in an exhibition budgerigar

The colours and markings of an adult budgerigar will vary according to each individual's colours and variety. All colours shown on a budgerigar at all times should be solid, pure and uniform in tone, with a nice sheen. Feather structure has a tremendous bearing on colour which is easy to maintain in small short tight feathered birds. However, when one sees large birds with increased

Two carved models created by R. Harris.

pattern thus giving a patchy appearance. Clearwings and the Black-eyed Yellows and Whites should not show signs of markings at all and it is a bad fault when they do.

Mask and cap
Mask and cap colours should be bright yellow or pure white although they are often dull yellow or greyish-white. Other faults are obvious signs of flecking and the encroachment of zebra markings on the cap.

Throat spots
The budgerigar should have six throat spots which are the same colour as a bird's markings and have a ground colour that is either yellow or white. All six spots should be approximately the same size. Too many spot feathers are unsightly and give an overcrowded appearance.

Opaline colours and markings
On most Opaline varieties the cap and its colouring should extend to a point on the back no lower than the wing butts, thus forming beyond this point a v-shaped area between the wings. The colour of this area is the same as the rest of the body. Usually, though, these areas are not clear of back, head and neck markings and as a result the bird has a mottled appearance. The back of head and neck colouring often become pronounced with bloom which is always regarded as a principal fault in an Opaline.

The wing feather markings should be the same as for all other colours and varieties of budgerigar although the ground colour should match that of the remainder of its body colour which, in this variety, will be distinctly opalescent. If, on the wing, the ground colour extends too far into the markings, taking away its symmetrical appearance, this is regarded as a fault.

Pied colours and markings
Pied markings on most varieties are either yellow or white and can be on any part of the body. Pied colouring should be in good contrast with the body colouring and markings and be evenly distributed. It can only be faulted when it is over- or under-emphasised.

Cheek patch and feet colour
Within the same colour and variety of bird there are great variations in the colour of the cheek patches and the feet.

numbers and size, these feathers will often lack colour on the tips. When the latter is visually close, tight and retain an evenness in colour tone with a nice sheen, this is a far better form of achievement.

You will learn from all standards that there are body colours in various colours of blue and green. Generally, body colour faults occur when the colour on the rump is not the same tone as the colour on the body. Colour fading on the chest, giving a patchy appearance, is quite common, and is more pronounced in Fallows.

Self-coloured birds such as Lutinos, Albinos and Black-eyed Yellows and Whites must be pure yellow or white. However, most of these varieties often have a green or blue suffusion which is most pronounced on the rump.

Markings
On varieties with wavy or zebra markings on the cheeks, back of head, neck and the wings, the markings vary in colour with the variety of bird — black in Normals, grey in Greywings and cinnamon in Cinnamons or Lacewings. Usually the ground colour is yellow or white.

A common fault with markings is when they are accompanied by bloom (body colour) or fade dramatically in tone. Fading is a fault more noticeable in Cinnamons or Greywings, particularly in the wings. Wing markings can also be irregular in their

Tail

Tail-feather colours should be well-defined.

Breeders and judges do not see the standard through the one pair of eyes and in practice this means that there are variations in the interpretation of the ideal. Perhaps it is just as well that this is so or after the first exhibition of the year the losers would not bother to exhibit any further. We must all agree that perfection in an exhibition budgerigar is represented by a bird that displays the perfect shape and stands on the perch in a correct position. This is necessary before its ideal conformation is able to be seen by all.

Judging

Judging has its rewards and any confrontations are usually outweighed by the enjoyable moments. A judge's biggest asset is his or her confidence in their ability and this only comes after many assignments. I doubt if any judge on their first few engagements is not a little unsettled by peering eyes. This feeling remains with some judges who, unfortunately, will never be accomplished in this field because during their commitments they will inevitably make some obviously wrong decisions while under pressure. The difficult task for a judge is to have complete insight into different varieties and for this reason I would agree with sound advice I was once given, 'You have to breed them to know them'. To sum up, therefore, a good judge is one who can place awards efficiently outside their own birdroom.

The task of judging budgerigars is never easy. Basically it involves the comparison of one bird with another and often one is confronted with many birds of different shapes and sizes which may be unsettled, and changing their pose every few seconds.

A budgerigar is essentially a bird of position and, at all times, the judge should be alert and watchful. Even the best trained birds may misrepresent themselves at times, therefore the judge must always allow a reasonable amount of time for each entrant to display its good and bad points, and to allow him or herself the opportunity to accurately assess their full potential. If one acts hastily the best bird in the show may be left without even a place card.

Procedure

Generally there is no set pattern to follow and most judges adopt their own method of procedure and placement of awards. These methods vary greatly so I will outline a plan that may be useful for a training judge.

Step 1

Make sure the birds are placed in a position that allows you to see them easily, preferably at eye level. Check to see that the number of birds stated on your class sheet is the same as the number before you.

Step 2

In all young or breeder's classes you should check that the ring worn on one leg is a recognised closed ring for that particular period of time. At the same time check the toes, legs and other parts for any malformations. Make sure the variety of bird is correct for the class stated on the schedule. Check the show cage to see if it complies with the required standard. You may have the steward remove any exhibit that has been eliminated. If you have noticed any sick birds present bring these to the attention of the chief steward so that they can be isolated.

Step 3

When you look through the class you may move to the head of the line any birds with type and uniformity. At the same time, if there is sufficient number in the class, birds out of condition or with obvious faults can also be eliminated.

Step 4

You can now begin to judge the whole bird. When a first, second and third decision is to be made you can eliminate birds by the shuffling process until you have what you consider the best four or five birds. The shuffling process consists of moving a bird around in a line so that they can be compared with the rest of the entrants. For example, the bird at the head of the line can be moved into No 2 position, No 3 position and so on down the line. The same procedure can be carried out with those remaining.

When you are confronted with a large class it is useful to judge them in two separate groups first. Have the steward bring the cages with the odd numbers. Take these for your first group and eliminate all but the first six placings, place this six aside. Then have the cages with the even numbers brought up and use the same procedure for them. Finally there will be twelve finalists and these can be judged as a single group in order to make your final placings.

Nearing the close of another successful exhibition, a judge, an exhibitor and an official take time out to relax.

This wing demonstrates depth in the markings with clearly defined white ground colour, depicting their early referrals as shell markings.

11 UPGRADING FEATURES OF THE EXHIBITION BUDGERIGAR

The foremost ambition of any breeder should be to obtain a quantity of fine stock. With this in mind he or she should be constantly striving for improvement in the features of their existing stock. If progress is to be made then the young produced should be superior in some ways to their parents. Ultimately, the production of a high class specimen will depend on the breeder's skill at selection combined with controlled breeding.

Reading matter will assist the exhibitor to improve and formulate ideas but if one is to derive any benefit from this information one should learn to listen, to look and to record.

Listening

Listen only to the people who have achieved results. That is, those who have, over many years, continually produced outstanding specimens from out of their birdrooms; or those who are perfectionists and have worked, also over a lengthy period, on programmes to bring some characteristic to the fore. It is by the efforts of these people that features are perfected and outstanding specimens produced.

Looking

Observe your own birds and those of others, in this way gaining a sense of what is good and bad in a budgerigar. Record these observations for easy reference when memory fails. If possible, make visits to breeders of note and achievement during the breeding season for then breeders cannot hide their selected matings and will proudly show the youngsters produced from them. Closely examine the parents, especially the hen, and note particularly the likeness of her daughter to herself, for these hens are the foundation for the perfection of any strain. At such times a photographic memory for family likeness is a great asset.

Recording

To be successful in any form of breeding, records must be kept, no matter how elaborate or simple the system may be. To serve any useful purpose, however, these must always be accurate, with detailed recorded observations of everything good or bad in every bird.

This recorded information is essential if we are to follow the ordered principles of inheritance in an effort to produce the variety or colour of your represented Ideal.

Objectives

The breeder who is breeding for a definite objective must plan years ahead. Whether it be for type, variety or colour, inferior features must be avoided or the sole object of your selections, that is, to maintain and bring together characters to enhance these features in your birds, may well prove ineffective. Therefore you should realise that both good and bad features in any visible or hidden form are ultimately regulated by percentages. Any youngster inherits fifty per cent of their genetical make-up from their father and fifty per cent from their mother. During fertilisation a blending process takes place, combining these percentages in the new offspring's genetical structure. Thus, if a poor bird is used its offspring will carry its poor features although these may remain part of its hidden genetical inheritance.

An example of this genetical inheritance is commonly seen in throat spots. If we were to pair two small-spotted birds together the expected result would be all small-spotted birds, however, when both parents have been bred from large-spotted parents we can expect to see twenty-five per cent of their young possessing the large spots of their grandparents. This see-sawing action, involving the visual and hidden genetical percentages, thus becomes quite evident and explains why a nest of offspring may vary greatly in every feature of their outward appearance and why no breeder can be sure of the resulting offspring.

Selection

Before commencing to breed you must have a

sound knowledge of your ideal budgerigar. Without this there is little hope of you ever selecting pairs suitable to produce such individuals. In any case, improvement in any feature can only be achieved slowly by selection which may only be possible in small degrees over a period of time. You will require great skill in selecting the birds with the highest degree of perfections in your initial stock. During this process individuals will be expected to transmit features they do not visually possess.

After years of skilful matings and ruthless culling you may possess the birds that are capable of commencing a strain. This will only occur when you are able to select individuals by their appearances. Their value can only be assessed by the offspring they can then produce. Any of these individuals, whose features closely resemble your ideal, can then be selected exclusively for the features they have been bred for. Nevertheless, one should always remember that no matter how well-bred a budgerigar is, it is still a combination of good and bad. Therefore, at all times observe carefully and consider thoroughly every aspect of their pedigree before you select your final pairing.

Breeding forms

Newcomers to specialist breeding will often encounter the terms — inbreeding, line-breeding and out-breeding. These forms of breeding are best described as the intelligent application of a few well-founded principles to enable one to produce any variety to the type and colour required. Of course in theory this seems to be a simple procedure; in practice it has many implications.

Inbreeding: the haphazard breeding of closely related birds, e.g. brother and sister.

Line-breeding: breeding undertaken with a pre-determined course in mind. It commences with the mating of a male and female not closely related. By careful selection over a period of time a bloodline is developed that carries fifty per cent of each of the original parents.

Both inbreeding and line-breeding have a purifying effect within the genes when correctly managed, thus bringing to the surface good, bad and indifferent features.

Figure 11. 1 Line breeding chart. Black represents the cock, white represents the hen.

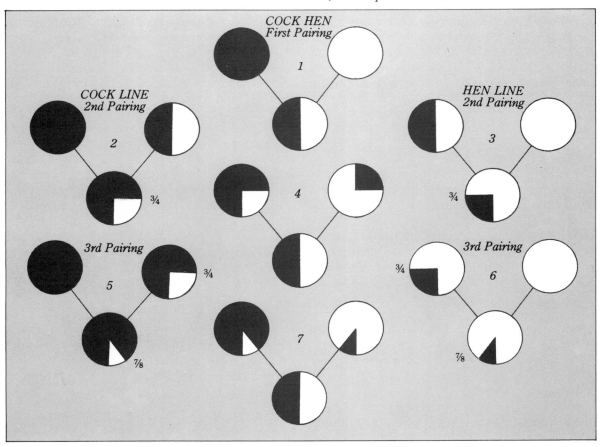

Out-breeding: breeding with two unrelated individuals. The result depends entirely on their genetical similarity so it is really a pairing of chance. Periodical forms of out-breeding take place in line-breeding to increase desirable features that are declining in a breeder's stock.

All three forms of breeding are ways of obtaining uniformity of desirable characteristics in your birds.

A simple method of line-breeding

One does not simply decide on the spur of the moment to line-breed and choose a cock and a hen for no apparent reason. On the contrary, having completed a breeding season and found that the progeny from a particular pair was of exceptionally high standard, and also free from what we might call the inferior bird, the breeder will have a reason to believe that these two birds have proven their worth as breeding stock.

In the next breeding season the highest quality young cock and hen produced from these parents will be chosen, although, because birds unfortunately die or have accidents just at the time you do not want them to, it is a sound practice to also keep the second best young cock and hen for reserves. The best cock bird is paired to its mother and the best young hen is paired to its father. The progeny of the original cock will carry three-quarters of his bloodline and one quarter of the original hen's, similarly, the progeny produced from the original hen will carry three-quarters of her bloodline and one quarter of the original cock bird. Only the best progeny from these matings should be retained.

Now, we must again select the best hen bird that was produced from the mating no. 2 (see Figure 11.1). This hen will carry three-quarters of the bloodline of the original cock bird, and on this occasion (pairing no. 5) is paired back to the original cock bird. Similarly, the best young cock has been retained from the pairing no. 3 and it is mated with the original hen (pairing no. 6).

This process, as outlined in Figure 11.1, results in the development of two predominant strains or bloodlines: one in which the progeny contain more and more of the cock's bloodline, the other in which the progeny contain more and more of the original hen's bloodline. At the same time, however, the breeder will also have been able to reproduce the youngsters in the first season.

If we take youngsters from pair no. 2 and mate them with partners from pair no. 3 we produce birds that carry fifty per cent of the original cock

and fifty per cent of the original hen, that is, pair no. 4. The process is also repeated after the third season, for if we intermate youngsters from pair no. 5 to those in no. 6 we again produce birds depicted in pair no. 7, which carry fifty per cent of the lines of the original cock and hen.

This exercise has involved the multiplication of the number of birds as well as the extension of the years of production of the youngsters far and beyond the time the original old pair could have been expected to reproduce so that, all going well, we could now have perhaps ten pairs of birds being mated together and breeding what we might call the fifty-fifty bird. In other words, the capacity of the original pair has been multiplied ten-fold. At the same time we have built up a reserve of birds that are, on the one hand, almost one hundred per cent of the original cock, and on the other, that are almost one hundred per cent of the original hen. This provides sound basis for the continuity of production in the following years.

There is only one real pitfall in this process, that is, if either the original cock or hen dies before three breeding seasons have passed, or if for some reason they fail to produce young in one of these seasons.

Breeding options

There is a natural tendency amongst all breeders of exhibition birds, and the budgerigar breeders are no exception, to try and produce a good big bird. It is comparatively easy to breed a smaller bird carrying the required characteristics and therefore, when the top class bigger bird appears, it is generally admired by all.

When two budgerigars are compared for shape and colour the difference in colour is seen by all even if the recognition of the lack of proportion may have to be learnt. Another very noticeable difference is that of feather structure. One bird's feathers may appear to be tight and short, while another's may be long and coarse. As an exhibition bird, the latter should not be tolerated.

In the breeding cage, we are often able to compensate for features that are undesirable and still produce worthwhile birds from stock that would not rate a place on the exhibition bench. Nevertheless, it should be stressed that any bird that is judged to be of poor or indifferent quality has no place whatsoever in any breeding establishment.

It would be an impossible task to set out a breeding pattern which could guarantee that a pair

A compatible group in a colony aviary.

of budgerigars could produce perfection in all the areas that make up the ideal bird. Thus in the selection of a new bird for the improvement of stock it will largely depend on the area that requires improvement whether one introduces a cock or a hen because there are some strains of birds where a particular feature displays itself strongly amongst one sex and is substantially weaker in the other. Thus, where a feature is weak in one sex it will be preferable to select a bird of the same sex in order to correct it. Obviously then, the new bird will have to excel in this character; even to a point of over-emphasis. For example, let us assume that a percentage of one's hens is lacking in head quality. We should then introduce a hen from a strain that excels in this character.

The advice that one should pair best to best, if followed indiscriminately may, in many instances, be ruinous. Best to best is all very well as long as the stock closely resembles the ideal in every way but to pair best to best from a stud where the two birds have a similar predominant fault will be non-productive.

In this instance matched pairs should be chosen and the best to best idea completely ignored. Matched pairs will provide a far better basis for selection to eradicate the predominating fault although, if the results are not satisfactory it may be necessary to break the pairs and choose another partner so that the season has not been wasted.

When one is aware of how many variations can control the shape of a bird, one soon realises that the breeder who continually produces birds of the correct shape has acquired tremendous skill. If, as well, the same breeder can consistently breed birds of the correct body size without any head, neck, wing and tail faults, with excellent colour and correct markings, further praise must be given for a superior achievement.

Fertility

Of all the requirements of any top strain of budgerigars there is nothing more important than the ability to reproduce in quantity. A stud of birds that may resemble the Ideal are completely useless if fertility is poor. Where this occurs and is not corrected the stud has a limited life. From the outset if would also seem essential to develop a group of hens that lay eggs in quantity. Some breeders are ruthless in this respect and will discard hens who constantly lay small clutches of eggs, regardless of how fine their physical appearance may be.

Once again, the reader should realise the importance of accurate record keeping, for it is useless to rely on memory in any of these matters. The shape of the eggs should also be noted so that one avoids developing a family of hens that produce eggs with perforated or irregular-shaped ends. This undesirable characteristic is the result of uneven shell distribution which often prevents further development prior to or during incubation. Any hen who constantly produces eggs of poor formation should be discarded, for hens with disorders of this kind become susceptible to egg-binding. Such instances can often be minimised by the choice of a hen with plenty of width between the legs — a feature many top breeders also look for.

If the breeder wishes to continue to use older hens it is not unusual to find that fertility will be reduced. However, anybody trying to establish a top stud should never reject the opportunity to pick up older birds from successful exhibitors for they are often of far better quality than the younger birds they can afford to sell. Even if the numbers of young produced is greatly reduced to as few as three or four from a season's pairing, these birds could later provide the foundation for a successful strain.

Large cock birds are often regarded as impotent when, in fact, their failure to produce may be caused by an inability to make physical contact in the proper manner. The choice of a hen that

Breeding results from this new mutation, Spangle, will certainly need to be recorded accurately.

appears flat in the pelvic region will often help the union to be made so that fertile eggs are produced.

Young hen birds of exceptional size often fail to reproduce because of their bulk. It is better to use such hens before they mature even though they may be normally regarded as being a little young.

Any reader who has seen films depicting the life cycle of the Caribou will vividly recall the struggle that occurs between the males prior to the mating season. In this manner nature provides that only the strongest, the fittest and most vigorous males reproduce. Likewise, the budgerigar breeder, with practice, can and should select his most vigorous cock birds to produce the young.

Feathers

Some features in an exhibition budgerigar will give it the appearance of being larger than birds seen before. This may puzzle the average fancier who does not often understand why it is so. A closer inspection, however, will reveal that this character is largely assisted by feather formation.

The effect that feather plays in the visual appearance of so many outstanding features in the exhibition budgerigar has not always been well enough understood. Any change in feather structure will change the outward appearance of the bird. When one begins to understand this important fact one should then study and understand the importance and the effect of yellow, buff and double buff feathers. The correct practice of mating yellow and buff-feathered birds is understood by all canary breeders, but because the different feather forms are more difficult to detect in budgerigars the inexperienced breeder may not be aware of their existence.

To the uninformed the reference to 'yellow' immediately brings to mind the colour of a bird but these terms — yellow, buff and double buff feathers — denote the structure of particular types of feather only. In each type these considerable differences in structure can sometimes be detected in the colour of the plumage.

Yellow

In the yellow form the feather will be fine, tight-webbed, and reveal a small amount of down at the base. The pigmentation will extend to the extreme edge of the feather and in such cases, when good body colour is evident, it is usually of a bright hue. The yellow feather is generally associated with the smaller, slim type of budgerigar.

Heavy down is generally associated with the better exhibition budgerigar.

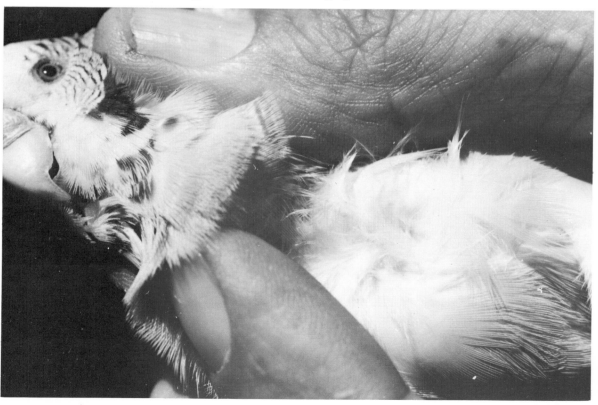

Buff

When we inspect a buff feather carefully the colour does not run to the edge. For this reason buff feathers often give an impression of reduced colour when in fact the external structure of the feather is responsible for this illusion.

The buff feather is noticeably longer than the yellow feather and has wider webbing; at the base there is a considerable amount of down. Also, a separate form of heavy down feathers may be present which spreads more or less evenly throughout the base of buff plumage.

Double buff

This form is as its name suggests and, as such, gives the bird an almost shaggy look. Moreover, the body colour may have a powdery appearance, a characteristic which is most evident in Lutinos. This form is also quite effective on wing markings, where it defuses and extends the ground colour.

There are many implications involved in breeding with the different types of feather but the recommended cross is always yellow to buff because it produces a more consistent equality in both size and feather. Excellent results can also be obtained by the mating of buff to buff although the advisabil-ity of this would be borne out by their pedigrees. On the other hand, the use of double buff birds should be undertaken with great caution in order to avoid feather abnormalities.

Longflight

Before any selective breeding pattern is explained regarding the implications of the separate wing forms, one's first concern should be to consult your Standard where one will find a description of the feather structure and required length of a normal wing.

The undesirable Longflight not only has abnormal length in both secondary and primary flight feathers but also has disorders in their numbers. This antagonism of length also persists in the tail feathers. For these reasons many fanciers, especially in Australia, have been plagued with problems with this aptly named bird and without the knowledge of the Mendelian pattern of this particular character the breeder may never hope to eliminate its continual appearance.

If one undertook the mating, Normal x Longflight, the resulting progeny would be another form called *intermediates*. Often these inter-

The comparisons for Yellow (top) and Buff feathers (bottom) were taken from the body (left) and shoulders (right).

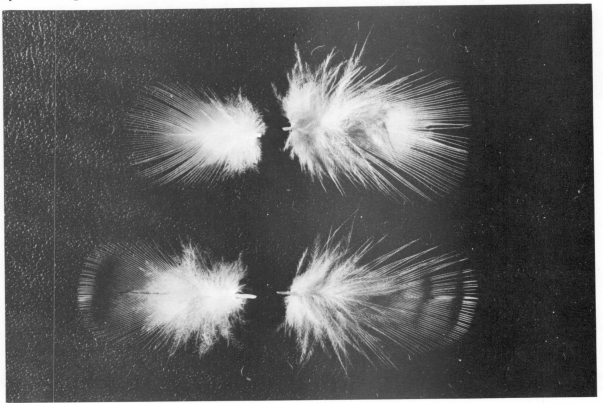

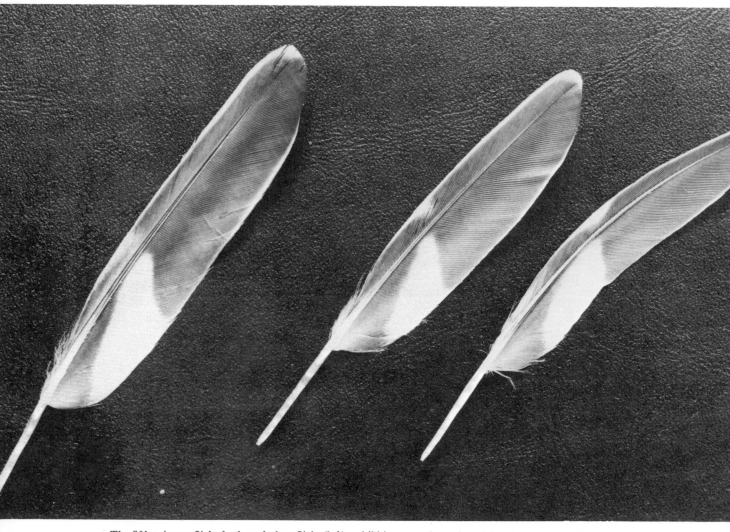

The fifth primary flight feather of a longflight (left), exhibition (centre), and a wild budgerigar (right), revealed a vast change in their structure.

mediates are difficult to distinguish, although birds with normal flight feathers often have overlarge secondary flight feathers and these, no doubt, are intermediate.

The breeding pattern of all three forms are comparable to the breeding of the colours: light (normal), medium (intermediate) and dark (longflight). Therefore, we will have to detect and select only normal forms for the elimination of any longflight influence. How does one determine the representative of the normal form? This individual displays a slight V-effect at a point where the ends of the secondaries overlap normal flight feathers.

The reduction of long tail feathers can only be perfected by the culling of such offenders, for

otherwise this character will persist in its appearance whenever such birds are mated.

Throat spots

A breeder once commented to me that this attractive and elusive feature was so difficult to produce and so easy to lose. Throat spots are not only controlled by inheritance, but also by the size and shape of the feathers on which they are displayed. Thus, if large spots are displayed on overlong mask feathers, their shape is distorted from circular to pear shape — they have the appearance of being drawn out even though the ground colour around their perimeter remains uniform.

There are two obvious patterns in which spots appear: one is a small spot (wild type), and the other is a mutation which increases the number and size of spots. Any breeders who have small spots

The throat spot (top left), is that of a wild budgerigar, alongside a nicely rounded exhibition throat spot. Below are others with numerous faults including odd shapes and sizes.

consolidated in their stock have an enormous task ahead of them to effect an improvement.

The Opaline variety was the first to show any noticeable improvement in the size of the six spots and these birds still prove a valuable asset when an increase in the size of spots is desired. In most instances a multi-spotted hen is your best selection, especially when pairing is with a bird that has the small spot. In such cases, whenever possible, introduce an Opaline with an excess of flecking up and over the neck. And, if you are aware of an Opaline in nest feather that is not unlike a Normal in the barrings, then retain this bird because, when matured, such birds are ideally suited for the improvement of *spots only*.

Faults appear when we see spots formed in various moon shapes or when the two inner spots are smaller than the others. These irregularities can only be rectified by pairing to ideally spotted birds.

A further fault is an excessive number of spots, often with slight lacing. These can only be reduced or controlled by selection, although a number of these are required in your stud, otherwise the stock will revert to the six small, dominant, spots of the wild budgerigar.

Mask

A good mask displays six nicely rounded, evenly-sized and evenly-spaced throat spots. To cultivate this feature, the use of a bird with a wide face will be necessary. The selected specimen should also exhibit a wide, deep mask that extends along the full length of the ear coverts and curves deeply to avoid the split appearance which so often occurs below the beak in short narrow-faced specimens.

Cheek patches

On wild budgerigars the cheek patches are triangular. This feature is of the utmost importance when perfecting the ornamental facial appearance of a budgerigar and special attention should be given to the pairing of birds if the shape is incorrect. On large-spotted birds the cheek patch should be wider at the bottom to enable it to cover half of the first spot.

Cap

The cap is often taken for granted but to be correct it should extend well back past the eye. The exception is the Opaline on which the colour should extend over the head and down to the wing butts, thus blending into and appearing as one with the mask. Flecking and the encroachment of the barrings into the cap are bad faults. The first signs of this are often detected commencing just above the eye.

Colour

The importance of colour in the body colour, ground colour and markings is aptly described and occasionally illustrated in colour charts in your ideal and any breeder trying to improve depth and colour in the budgerigar will be confronted with many variations. In addition, each colour does not always develop uniformly throughout the plumage and when we attempt to breed Clearwings, Black-eyed Yellows and Whites, the dark colours of the markings, which we are trying to eliminate, will usually linger, becoming more and more pronounced after every moult.

The fancier, while endeavouring to intensify colour, may also introduce some undesirable character. Even so, good colour is by no means dominant over bad colour, no more than poor colour is dominant over good colour, and when good and poor colour are combined the result will be a medium colour. This applies equally to the colour of the body markings and the ground colour.

Pigmentation is an inherited character which, because it is visual, is the easiest of all factors to improve. The first object should be to produce purity in colour for without this we will achieve nothing. Occasionally we see quite obvious variations in colour intensity due simply to an uneven inter-action during the development of the colour pigmentation. Plumage colours of this kind often lack intensity and appear paler in certain parts, for example, the plumage on the chest of a green bird might be diluted yellow.

Obvious exhibition faults of this bird are flecking in the cap, together with multi-spots protruding too far down the mask.

Another colour fault is the heavy hue of another colour seen on many medium and dark coloured birds. Both are faults in pigmentation that are transferable to their offspring, therefore, their use should be curbed if evenness of colour is required.

The effect of evenness in body colour can be judged best by examining the colour on the bird's rump and chest: they should be the same. In the markings the quality of the colour is determined by examining the wing tips and throat spots. From these four points you will be able to ascertain the standard of an individual bird's colour constitution. The purity and evenness of colour necessary in a first class bird of exhibition colour are achieved by

selection, and the elimination of its inhibitors are
only possible by degrees.

On the other hand, many breeders often obtain
good results with the use of the cinnamon gene,
which gives a soft yet brightly distinctive plumage
colour (especially in Black-eyed Yellows) that is
influenced by the bird's inability to manifest cinnamon colour. Also, offspring from the mating
Normal/Cinnamon cock x Cinnamon hen will yield
some hens as Normals, although the possession of
purity and evenness in their plumage will have been
determined by the inherited feather constitution of
their parents.

Depth of colour

When we consider increasing the depth of colour it
is important that all birds used should have exceptional colour. Because of a link between the body
colour and mask colour we should select individuals
with the deepest and clearest yellow or white mask
in order to develop further the deeper colours.

Undesirable faults often appear first in the
markings where an infusion of colour in some
specimens may be found. A frequent offender is
one which is often incorrectly referred to as bloom.
This suffusion of body colour begins by encroaching
into the ground colour of the head and wing
markings, an occurrence often believed to be an
inherited consequence of breeding depth of colour
but this belief is disproved by the evidence that
poor coloured specimens exhibit the same variations. A further problem is patchiness, especially on
wing markings, which is due to an overriding colour
suppression.

None of these characteristics should be allowed
in any pairing when undertaking to breed for
perfection. What are required are birds with
striking intensifications, with markings that appear
clear and well-defined, their striations neat and
narrow.

The difference between the hereditary constitution of a male and female is that the colour of her
markings will be lighter. Therefore, whenever
depth is desirable the darkest markings procurable
on a hen should be used — in the vast majority of
cases these will be found on grey or violet factor
birds.

As the reader can see, the production of colour is a time-consuming, although rewarding, business. Nevertheless, the best colour features will not be recognised if a bird is not groomed properly. When this is done its feathers should have a bright sheen.

Type

The features that should be considered when choosing a budgerigar for breeding purposes will be apparent when the subject is standing at the correct angle on the perch. Thus, when selecting for type breeding one should look for the birds that display an inherited steadiness. In this respect one will have to distinguish between show birds and aviary birds: for example, your records will reveal that a particular bird stands out like a champion in the aviary but fails dismally in outline when placed in a show cage. On the other hand, it is also advisable to consider those birds that appeared unstable in the nest — they could change with maturity. A good policy in breeding is to avoid selecting any birds with a disfigured or poor outline.

Size

Fanciers trying to produce ideal size are breeding simultaneously for ideal length and proportion and, while there are approved length limits of a budgerigar, proportion relates more to personal taste than to any calculated drawing of a specimen. Therefore, it is the fancier's conception of perfection that determines their dedication to slight modifications, whether they be devoted to making a specimen's shape larger or smaller.

Increased size is purely a hereditary factor and provided it is not prejudicial in any way to a budgerigar's appearance or well being, there is little that can be said against it.

It is possible for a breeder to cultivate improved size from two small birds whose parents were much larger. Theoretically, one in four of their progeny will have the larger size, but because this law applies over many hundreds of pairs and this sample is too small to guarantee genetic expectations it is advisable to have available birds that have inherited the longer skeleton that accompanied the Longflight mutation. In addition, one will also need a bird with an obviously good frame, that is, a robust big boned specimen. Its usefulness in this respect is often indicated by its large feet, which occasionally have signs of feathers at the top of the claws.

Attention should also be given to the skull which should display prominence of width and height. If only one such bird has been obtained, the best advice is to select the young that have eyebrows of down when in the nest feather because these birds will undoubtedly carry, visually or hidden, more of this desired character.

Generally, however, the selecting process should be combined with good husbandry and excellent conditions and adequate caring for stock will produce worthwhile results.

Beak and frontal rise

There is nothing that looks worse than a beaky exhibition budgerigar. This factor is undoubtedly tied in with frontal rise: a beaky bird gives the impression it has been cut off over the cere. A bird with this obviously bad fault should never have a place in any breeding programme. The type of bird that should have a place has a beak that is neat but not thin and is tucked into the face. The less obvious it is, the better the frontal appearance will be.

Also, the head of a hen may be a little squatter in its appearance than a cock but on both the feather above the cere should appear to project outwards as well as upwards.

Back skull

An excellent back skull is quite noticeable on a budgerigar even at the age of five days. A combination of the breadth of the bone structure and feather structure give this form its expression. Thus, its production is based purely on detection and selection: discard any bird that appears to have been sliced away at the back of the head.

Eye

The correct positioning of the eye is vital to a feeling of balance in a bird. The eye of any bird selected should not be central but noticeably closer to the beak. The centre of the eye should run parallel with the top of the cere. The eye itself should not be slanted, a shape often detected in the early development of flat-headed individuals and is sometimes confused with the eye that is well set into the face. The latter creates the appearance of a heavy brow, a prominent feature on many ideal breeding specimens.

Neck

A nip in the neck is one of an exhibition budgerigar's worst failings because its presence breaks the clean outline of the back. The use of such birds should be discontinued because their influence will quickly spread through a breeder's

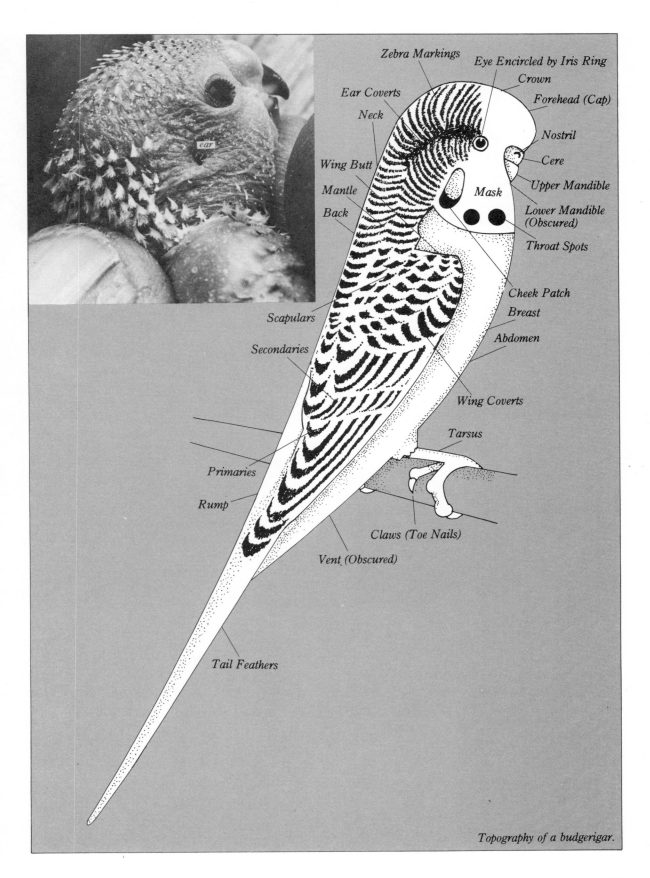

ear

Zebra Markings

Eye Encircled by Iris Ring

Crown

Ear Coverts

Forehead (Cap)

Neck

Nostril

Wing Butt

Cere

Mantle

Mask

Upper Mandible

Back

Lower Mandible
(Obscured)

Throat Spots

Scapulars

Cheek Patch

Breast

Secondaries

Abdomen

Wing Coverts

Tarsus

Primaries

Rump

Claws (Toe Nails)

Vent (Obscured)

Tail Feathers

Topography of a budgerigar.

This Cinnamonwing is a form of longflight and also has a smudgy heavy ground colouring. These are not desirable.

A specimen of a good Normal wing.

stock. This undesirable feature is the result of a narrow neck which makes the head and beak appear out of proportion. For this reason, the bird with a deep, thick neck that gives it an unbroken backline from the top of the head down the body should be chosen.

Body

An ideal body would show a nice rotundity and have a streamlined profile from the head and neck to the tail. The breast bone should not appear projected and give the impression of a keel. If it does, eliminate this type of bird. Other problems are

shallowness and chestiness, which completely disrupt the rhythm of the frontal line.

A good backline often accentuates a pleasing head and neck — an effect that is destroyed by a scooped back and too high rump in birds that are short and dumpy. At the other extreme, long birds often give the impression of being tubular and drawn out.

When pairings are taking place the correct body features seem more essential in the cock bird than the hen. However, this does not mean that they should be neglected in the hen.

Short bodies can be compensated for by pairing

the aviary or flight cage but tips the wings under pressure in the show cage should not be treated in this way. Obviously, in the latter case, the action is only a result of nervousness and may never show itself in any of the offspring.

The second major wing fault that completely spoils the bird's outline is where one or both wings are dropped down at the sides of the body. The wings appear to be held loosely and, even if the bird is stirred up mechanically, it is still unable to hold them in the correct manner. These birds should also be discarded.

Some readers may wonder at the consistent culling of any bird that exhibits the abovementioned faults, however, most breeders who have bred budgerigars over a number of years cannot but be very aware of the futility of attempting to breed out inherited faults.

Tail

The line from the back of the neck to the tip of the tail should appear to be straight, yet, if it was completely so it would not look right. The truth of the matter is that the tail kicks slightly upwards to give the bird balance and the illusion of a straight line down the back.

This balance is lost if the bird continually carries its tail in a dropped position, that is, has what is called 'a dropped tail' — another trait that should not be tolerated in any bird in the breeding cage.

Position

This relates to stance and balance: a budgerigar that continually lays across the perch has no place in the breeding programme. Those that have a banana-shaped carriage are also useless for the production of the exhibition budgerigar.

Lack of steadiness can be rectified with training and is usually only a display of nervousness, however, one occasionally finds a bird that does not quieten to the show cage whatever the degree of training and such a bird should be treated with the greatest caution when breeding.

Balance

No one appreciates the importance of balance more than the breeder of top class exhibition canaries. No canary can stand correctly in position and offer a proportionate and pleasing appearance to the eye unless it carries as much of its body behind the legs as in front. Length of tail is not the answer, the

with long bodies; and shallowness can be altered by pairing with good depth. Hens, with age, appear a little irregular in shape, so this is a point that has to be considered also. An ideal stock hen should give the impression of broadness.

Wings

Two faults that completely spoil the appearance of the exhibition budgerigar are found in the wing carriage. Firstly, a good bird is completely ruined by the continual crossing of the wing flights. Birds that have this habit must be discarded, although the bird that normally displays correct wing carriage in

canary breeder is looking for depth in the area from the underside of the wings through to the tail flights. If the bird does not conform in this manner it is usually described as being cut up into the vent or wedge-tailed, referring to its overall appearance of being chopped off behind the legs.

The breeder of budgerigars has to aim to provide the same sense of balance. If the bird chops off sharply behind the legs and does not come through with sufficient length it is out of balance, and cannot stand in position. The inability to display a good outline and hold the correct position because of a lack of balance makes the bird virtually worthless.

Legs

At first glance, the legs on an exhibition budgerigar seem to provide little reason for comment. To so many breeders they command little or no attention. We have spoken about position, balance, outline, carriage, and of course no bird can depict these qualities unless the total complement of leg position and length is correct.

Legs should not be placed too wide apart on the perch otherwise the body will be closer to the perch than is desired and so appear squat. A good set of legs should show a little thigh and give the bird the right amount of definition.

On the odd occasion where the bird shows too much thigh, it will appear long-legged and its outline will be disrupted. It would be wise for the breeder to keep this in mind when selecting stock.

Conclusion

In contrast to the wild budgerigars, which appear to us to be unvarying, the exhibition breeder's birds vary greatly. Not only in one particular breeder's aviary, but also from breeder to breeder. The reason for this is that, in contrast to nature, each individual breeder has made his or her own selective pairings.

This same breeding procedure is undertaken by countless thousands of fanciers all over the world who are also in a transitional stage of development of one or any number of features.

Whether it be for type, variety or colour the sensible task for an exhibitionist would be to go into every breeding season with an idea of what next year's future opposition is likely to be. Your first concern then, in any short or long term breeding programme, would be pedigree. This, combined with fitness and quality may help you to progress in the desired direction.

There will always be fanciers who, after several years of breeding, will obtain better results than others who, during the same period, have been breeding with birds of like origin. Two factors are involved here — they are ability and dedication.

When one considers the books that have been written on the subject covered in this chapter, the reader must realise that the information presented here is very condensed. Nevertheless, it does provide a basis for one to set out a programme for the present time.

Records of the experiences of individuals who have spent an enormous amount of time and effort studying and improving any number of the features mentioned here are often available for one to read in the journals put out by the various budgerigar societies and in *Cage and Aviary Birds*, the English weekly publication on this subject.

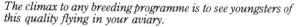

The climax to any breeding programme is to see youngsters of this quality flying in your aviary.

12 VARIETIES AND COLOURS

Budgerigars are classified by variety and colour. For example, the name *Greywing Sky Blue,* refers to the variety and colour of an individual bird. Before we can understand any procedure for the purchasing, or breeding of any particular bird, we should first have an understanding of the colourations of the many different varieties and colours of budgerigars existing today.

Colour plates within this book show distinct variations of these colourations. The birds shown are outstanding exhibition specimens of their particular variety and colour and the characteristics displayed by these birds denote purity in breeding which every budgerigar does not possess. For this reason, the colourations of many birds may be quite inferior to that shown.

Most birds, however, will possess obvious features and the following is a summary of the characteristics of the many varieties and colours of the budgerigar.

Some varieties can be distinguished by their markings, that is, the feathers which appear as wavy markings on the head, back, neck and wings. Throat spot feathers are usually the same colouring as the markings, too. The feathers, which make up the markings and throat spots, are all individually edged or striped (as in the zebra markings) with definite colour which is generally referred to as the *ground colour.* A bird's ground colour is usually more pronounced on the facial features — the cap and the mask, although the varieties of budgerigars known as the Opalines and Yellow-face Blues are the exceptions to this rule.

Plumage colour is the guide to the *colour* of the bird, for example: in a Greywing Sky Blue — greywing indicates the *variety,* and sky blue, the plumage colour and *colour.* In some cases, the plumage colour may indicate the variety also, for example, in Yellows, the bird is of the Yellow variety when it possesses a black eye. Plumage colour is usually referred to as *body colour.*

On some mature budgerigars the variety and colour can only be correctly determined by a close inspection of the cere, which is normally blue on the cock and brown on the hen; or the eye, which is normally black with a white iris ring. Variations in colour in the cheek patches and in the two main tail feathers, may be an important clue while, at times, a close inspection of the shafts of the main tail feathers will be necessary.

In most cases, however, you will find that the title given to the variety or colour of the bird is obviously appropriate.

Normals

All budgerigars classified as Normal retain the black feather markings found on the typical wild green budgerigar. They will also have six prominent ornamental throat spots on the mask.

A Normal in the Green series can be Light Green, Laurel or Dark Green, Olive or Grey-green. In the Blue series a Normal can be Sky Blue, Cobalt, Violet, Mauve or Grey.

On a Green series bird the ground colouring, mask and the cap will be yellow, and on the Blue series the ground colour, mask and cap will be white.

Eye
Black pupil with a white iris ring.

Tail
Tail feather quills are black on all Normals and the remainder of the feather is shown in various shades of blue-black colouring, with the exception of Grey-greens and Greys which have completely black feathers both in the tail and in all the markings.

Feet
Greyish-black.

Cheek patches
All cheek patches are violet shades in Greens, Blues, Yellows and Whites; and grey in Grey-greens and Greys, unless otherwise stated.

Body colour
Greens
1 *Light Green:* Varies from a rich grass-green to a yellowy green.
2 *Laurel or Dark Green:* Deep grass-green to the colour of the laurel leaf. A deep blue colouring is superimposed on this intense body colour in the area above and below the rump.
3 *Olive:* Light to deep olive-green. Often accompanying the colour of blue.
4 *Grey-green:* May be light, medium or dark grey-green, or vary from a mustard-green to a deep olive grey-green.

Blues

1 *Sky Blue:* May vary from a powder-blue to a deep sky-blue.
2 *Cobalt:* The body colour of a Cobalt is as its name suggests, however, these birds may be lighter in colour around the chest.
3 *Violet:* Various shades of violet.
4 *Mauve:* A dark purplish mauve which is often accompanied by a lighter cobalt.
5 *Grey:* There are light, medium and dark forms and tones range from a light, bluey-grey to a deep, solid grey.

Yellows

The body colour, markings and tail feathers of a Yellow range from light lemon to a deep yellow. Green suffusion in various shades may be visible, especially on the rump. Markings and throat spots may be apparent but only on poor specimens. Cheek patches may vary in colour from dull violet shades to white, although Grey-yellows have bluish-grey patches. The pupil of the eye is black with a white iris ring, hence the name, Black-eyed Yellows.

Whites

Whites generally have a strongly suffused blue appearance, although Grey-whites are a dull grey. Markings and throat spots tend to be more pronounced on Whites than Yellows. Cheek patches and eye colours are the same as in Yellows, thus Whites are generally referred to as Black-eyed Whites.

Lutinos

When colour suppression occurs in the form of albinism in any Green or Yellow budgerigar it is given the name Lutino. In Lutinos the pupil of the eye is red with a white iris ring and the cere of the cock is purplish flesh coloured. The hen's cere ranges in colour from light to nut-brown. Cheek patches vary from a dull violet to a pale blue. The body colour, markings, and tail feathers range from lime-yellow to a deep buttercup and the rump and body colour may have a green sheen. Flights and the main tail feathers may be more white than yellow; feet and legs are pink.

Albinos

Albinism of any Blue or White budgerigar will produce Albinos but on a Yellow-face the facial feature remains quite visible. Cheek patches vary in colour from pinkish-violet to pure white. The body colour, markings and tail feathers range from white, heavily suffused by blue colouring, to a white which is occasionally tinged with brown. Eye, cere and feet colour are the same as in Lutinos.

Greywings

The markings and six ornamental throat spots on this variety are grey. The Greywing can be combined with any of the Green and Blue series and when this is done their ground colouring, mask and cap remain yellow and white, respectively. The Greywing is also combined with Black-eyed Yellows and Whites. In these combinations the ground colouring is yellow and white respectively.

While the colour markings of a Greywing are quite well-defined on most Blue, Yellow and White series birds, they may be less so in combinations with birds that have a dark green body colour. The tail feathers are grey with a bluish tinge, except in the Greys and Grey-greens where the bluish tinge is missing.

Clearwings

In this variety the ground colour completely envelopes the colour of the markings. This is a very attractive feature when it is combined with any of the Green and Blue series birds. With Greens, the mask, cap, ground colour and wing markings are yellow and the tail feathers are pale green. With Blues, the mask, cap, ground colour and wing markings are white and the tail feathers are pale blue.

Grey factor Clearwings, Greys and Grey-greens may show a tinge of grey in the tail feathers also. Grey markings and grey throat spots may be quite noticeable: the problem then is to determine whether a bird is a poor Clearwing or a light Greywing.

Cinnamonwings

In Cinnamonwings the markings and six ornamental throat spots are affected by a genetic suppression of their normal black colouring. An added effect is the dilution of body colour — clearly seen when it is combined with any of the Green of Blue series birds although the ground colour, mask and cap remain yellow and white respectively. Similarly, when Cinnamonwings are combined with Black-eyed Yellows and Whites the ground colours are yellow and white respectively. The tail feather quills are brown and the rest of the feather is in various shades of blue, with the exception of Grey-greens, Greys,

Yellows and Whites which have cinnamon colouring. The pupil of a Cinnamonwing is red for its first week of life and after that it is black with a white iris ring. Feet and legs are flesh pink.

Lacewings

Lacewings are a composite of the Cinnamonwing and the Lutino or Albino. Therefore body colours, cheek patches, ceres, eyes and feet will be identical to that of the Lutino or Albino. As with the Cinnamonwing the ground colouring is yellow on the Lutino form and white on the Albino form. A distinctive feature in a lightly coloured Lacewing is that the two main tail feather quills are brown.

Opalines

The special feature of the Opaline is the lack of prominent markings on the back, neck and head. The Opaline's mask and cap colour should extend over the back and merge into the body colour at a point level with the wing butts. At this point the markings should cease completely, thus leaving a clear V-effect between the tops of the wings and the centre of the back. The markings on the wings and the six ornamental throat spots retain the colour of the composite variety or colour represented but the ground colour in the wings is the same as the body colour, thus giving the bird its opalescent character.

Opalines can be combined with any Green or Blue series bird, as well as Black-eyed Yellows and Whites. They are also paired with Normals, Greywings, Clearwings, Cinnamonwings and Lacewings.

Pieds

A Pied budgerigar is easily recognisable, especially when the pied markings are prominent. Any bird that has a clear area of colour foreign to the particular variety or colour is regarded as being a pied, for example, a clear area of yellow on a Green series bird or white on a Blue series bird. These pied markings are due to a lack of black pigmentation in the feathers and skin (noticeable on the feet) where the pied markings occur.

The mechanics of suppression of colour in all Pieds is the same although the distribution of pied areas varies — many having variegated body markings and others have variegated wings. Quite often birds with both these characteristics are seen, although some will have neither to any great extent. Tail and flight feathers can be pied marked but it is not unusual to see only one flight or tail feather showing this characteristic. Throat spots and cheek patches may even be partially or completely eliminated by the pied area.

There are several different Pied varieties, each of which has its own characteristic. It is my intention to deal with only the most familiar of these varieties here. Thus, for the sake of simplicity and because the eye colour and cheek patches are the same as in any of the non Pied varieties the following explanations will only concern a Pied in a Normal Light Green bird.

Australian Dominant Pied

This variety of Pied frequently carries a head spot (a small pied marked area) which was also evident on the first mutation of this variety.

The pupil is black with a white iris ring and the cheek patches are violet, unless suppressed by pied markings. Legs and feet are grey-black unless pied areas are evident, in which case they will be flesh-pink.

Dutch Dominant Pied

The Dutch Pied is similar in appearance to the Australian Pied, however, there are variations in some features.

The pupil is black and may or may not have the white iris ring in one or both eyes. The cheek patches are always white, or violet and white. The legs and feet are flesh-pink, or grey-black and flesh-pink.

Danish Recessive or Harlequin Pieds

The pied area and body colour on this Recessive Pied is a clear bright shade and, on the hen, the markings are usually darker. Blurred markings will often be evident, being more pronounced on the wing. The pupil is black without the usual white iris ring. Cheek patches are white; legs and feet are flesh-pink. The cere on the cock is flesh-coloured and on the hen, light to nut-brown.

Yellow-face

The yellow face of this variety is only a facial character that can transmit its form onto any colour or variety of budgerigar. Yellow-faces have two forms: Type 1, which displays more of a creamy face; and Type 2, which is prominent in Australia and has a bright yellow face. Both types are prominently displayed on any of the Blue or White series birds, however, various shades of green body colour may be evident at times. The yellow facial colouring may also extend into the ground

Normal Grey-Green cock.

Normal Grey cock.

Normal Sky Blue cock.

Black-eyed Yellow hen.

Spangle Laurel
(Dark Green) cock.

Yellow-face Sky Blue cock.

Australian Dominant Pied
Grey-Green cock.

Crested Cinnamonwing
Light Green cock.

colouring, especially in the wing markings.

Fallows

Any variety or colour of budgerigar can be a Fallow. The Fallow is a result of an altered factor which produces reddish, yellow or brownish eumelanin in place of the normal black. As a result, Fallows are characterised by pastel shades in their represented colourations with more pronounced body colour on and below the rump. Also markings may be patchy in appearance, especially on the wings.

The eye has clear red pupils with a white iris ring with the exception of the English Fallow which has clear red pupils without a visible iris ring. The cere of the cock is flesh-coloured and the hen's cere is light to nut-brown. The beak is orange and the legs and feet are flesh-pink. Tail feathers are brown but have a bluish tinge at times.

Spangles

The Spangle can superimpose its character onto any variety or colour of budgerigar but is not visual on Yellows or Whites. It has made its introduction as a result of the reversal of the normal pigment cells and feather forming cells. The best visible example of this reversal is when the bird is only a Single Factor Spangle. Then, say in a Normal Green bird, the throat spot feathers will look like targets, that is, black with a yellow centre.

In the Spangle what was the original ground colour of the variety becomes the colour of the markings and vice versa. The tail feathers also reflect this reversal of colours, although it is not unusual to occasionally have odd markings on the tail feathers of any bird. The cere, feet, eye, mask, cap and body colours of a Spangle remain identical to the variety or colour reproduced although cheek patches may be divided into shades of the represented colour, for example, half-white and half-violet on a Sky Blue.

Double Factor Spangles
The Double Factor Spangles that have been recently produced appear in any variety of the Green and Blue series birds. In nest feather these birds give the appearance of a perfect specimen of a Black-eyed Yellow or White and show no visible evidence of their inherited Spangle markings. When these birds attain their adult plumage their body colour appears to be in the same as a heavily suffused Black-eyed Yellow or White. Markings, especially on the wings, will also be evident, albeit unpronounced.

Crested

The Crested bird can show its character on any variety or coloured budgerigar. Their title is derived from the appearance of an actual crest which varies in shape from a simple tuft at the front of the head to a full crest. This form can also be apparent on other parts of the body where it is seen as an abnormal feather growth.

Combination

From all the previously mentioned varieties and colours there are many combinations that are able to be reproduced. Some common ones are Cinnamonwing Opalines and Greywing Opalines. From a combination of three varieties, Yellow-face, Opaline and Clearwing, we can produce a composite form called Rainbows. Although Rainbows are produced in all of the Blue series birds, they are more pleasing to the eye in the lighter shades — Sky Blue, Cobalt or Violet. When one considers that we may venture a little further even and produce Rainbow Pieds one begins to realise that the combinations possible are endless.

Half-siders or Bi-colours

These birds are made up of split combinations of either variety or colour and, at times, both. Their reproduction cannot be determined or controlled in the usual manner: they are freak birds, a result of a breakdown within the orderly cell divisions during the process of reproduction.

The best presentation of Half-siders is when each side, representing a bird of a different colour, is separated by a dividing line running down the centre of the bird, for example, Green on one side and Blue on the other. It is more usual however, for a small portion of one side to reveal signs of a different colour or markings.

There have been cases of Bi-colours reproducing their kind. In one case these birds were Normal Sky Blues which had a band of green colouring running across the chest, and over a period of four seasons a number of reproductions had occurred with the intensity of this green colouring across the chest increasing notably. This is by no means a comprehensive list of the varieties and colours in existence. There are many others that are rarely seen at present and it is possible that someday these may become popular, perhaps as a result of their use with known or new mutations to create a new variety or colour. Despite their rarity, these birds, along with other newcomers, will continue to be included in the budgerigar's nomenclature.

13 MUTATIONS

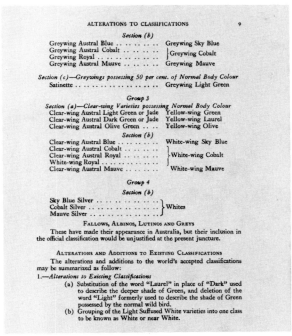

Vernacular names changed to their correct nomenclature by the Australian Budgerigar Council in 1936.

When Charles Coxen gave his brother-in-law, the famous naturalist, John Gould, a pair of wild green budgerigars, which were subsequently transported to England in 1840, little did he realise what a tremendous impact these birds were to have throughout the world. Today, it seems incredible that these two green birds have evolved into so many colours.

The wild budgerigar originated from the combination of pairs of genes that resulted in the visual colour we now call Light Green. All other colours and varieties that have occurred since are the result of mutation, that is, changes that have occurred within the gene structure (see the chapter, The Laws of Inheritance).

Strange though it may seem, when birds are in captivity some mutations make an almost simultaneous appearance in different parts of the world. Moreover, it is not unusual to find that the greatest

numbers occur in the country of the origin of the species.

Unfortunately, however, data concerning the parentage of new mutations is often unknown because of lack of observation and records. In other instances it is withheld by the jealous owner. In these cases there are no means of tracing their genetic tree to establish their origin. Thus, the breeder who provides records and breeding history does the bird fancy a great service.

The colour of the early mutations would not be unlike those still appearing in birds in the wild. The difference is that the mutation that occurs in captivity is treasured, and treated with great acclaim. This results in concerted efforts to produce more and in a short time the quality improves and the standard for a new variety is established.

In the wild the mutation that occurs receives no such special treatment. More often than not its occurrence makes the bird more susceptible to predators and, for this reason, mutations in the wild have not often been noted. The following observation, made in 1947, is an exception.

> Early on the morning of July 30 large flocks watered at Duchess Dam and I noticed one bird that was bright yellow in colour. This bird stood out conspicuously from the others as they wheeled in the early morning sun.[1]

The first pair of Wild Green budgerigars that were sold in London in the early 1840s fetched twenty-six English pounds. This was very reasonable compared to the prices paid later for mutations. In the early 1920s when particular mutations were in their early development, prices in Europe varied from 100 to 500 English pounds for a pair.

In Sydney in 1927, Japanese buyers were reported to have paid £125 or $250 for pairs of Sky Blues — certainly high prices in that era. Australian Pied budgerigars were readily sought for undisclosed sums by American ex-servicemen returning home at the end of the Second World War. More

Recessive Pied Sky Blue hen.

Opaline Cinnamonwing
Sky Blue hen.

Cinnamonwing Grey-Green cock.

Opaline Grey-Green hen.

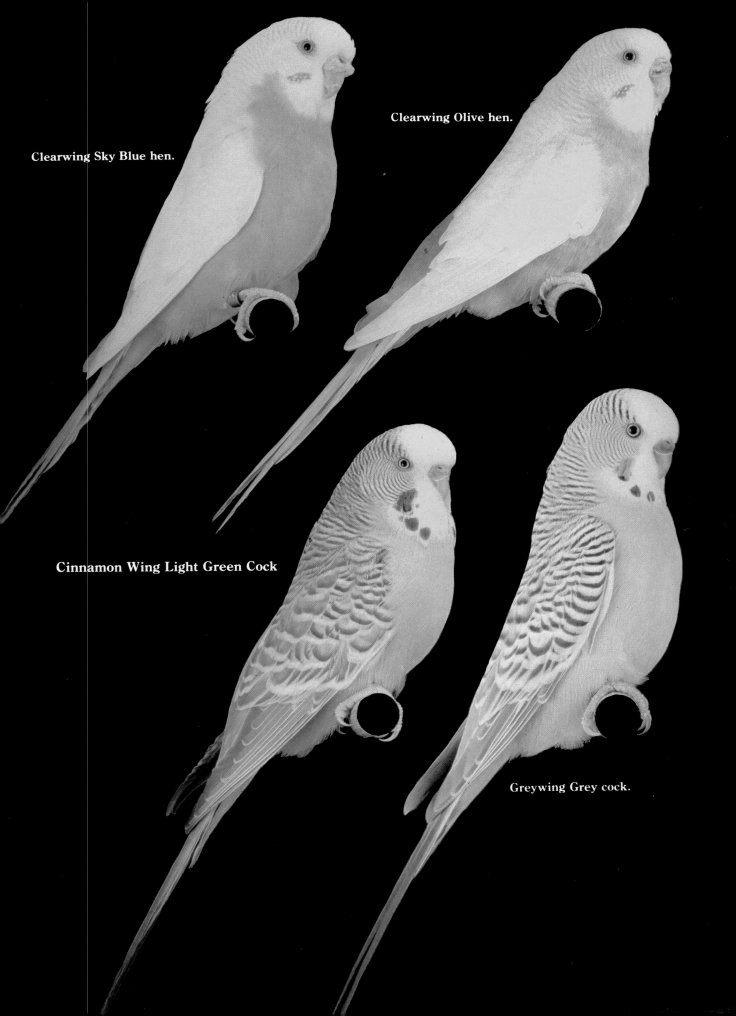

Clearwing Sky Blue hen.

Clearwing Olive hen.

Cinnamon Wing Light Green Cock

Greywing Grey cock.

recently, prices paid for Australia's newest mutation, the Spangle, have reached $200 locally. These birds have now been transported to Europe where they should command an even higher figure.

Budgerigar mutations can be exported legally from Australia but the ban placed in 1935 on the exporting of Wild Greens still remains in force. Overseas mutations, however, cannot be imported into Australia because of strict quarantine regulations.

From early records the colour of Yellow was the first mutation to make its appearance in captivity. This occurred in Belgium in 1872. These Yellow budgerigars, with black eyes, were not introduced into Australia until 1900.

The colour Sky Blue also appeared in Belgium in 1878 and gave budgerigar breeders an entirely new direction in the production of new colours. When exhibited in London in 1910 they created a sensation and took a strong hold on the imagination of fanciers. The first Sky Blues were shipped from Europe to Australia in 1918.

English importers observed Dark Greens (Laurels) amongst batches of imported Wild Greens in 1915 and it is interesting to note that this colour is often recognised in wild flocks in Australia.

Olives were produced from Dark Greens in 1916. Shortly after, Cobalts and Mauves were also developed with the help of Dark Green birds.

Greywings were known to have appeared in 1875 in Belgium but were not firmly established in England until 1920. The most attractive of all the Greywings, the Greywing Yellow was first developed by J. Shaw of Sydney in 1934.

In 1930 the first Clearwing appeared and was developed in the aviaries of H. Pier of Sydney. There too, in later years, H. Yardley cultivated this beautiful mutation to perfection. The Clearwing was exported and the first early examples, Royal Austral Blues (Whitewing Cobalts), were presented to King George V in 1934.

Lutinos existed in Europe in 1880 but then disappeared to reappear simultaneously in Europe and Australia between 1932-36.

Albinos evolved later from the use of Lutinos and birds of blue colouring.

Fallows, which seemed to be partly nocturnal, appeared in the aviaries of Mr B. O'Brien in Sydney in 1930: they also appeared in Europe about this time.

An Opaline was discovered amongst a consignment of wild budgerigars at the Adelaide market in 1933. It was a green hen, in baby plumage, and it passed into the hands of S. Terrill of Adelaide. Like the Dark Greens, the Opalines have been observed in wild flocks and in 1934 an Opaline hen was bred in England, apparently from imported Wild Greens.

The appearance of Cinnamonwings in Australia in 1933 also coincided with reported appearances in Europe, although they had been known to be in existence for some time. In recent times Cinnamonwings were sighted in wild flocks in western New South Wales. One such female was caught and on close inspection was found to be a Cinnamon Green. It exhibited all the wild budgerigar's characteristics.

Where and when the first Violet was produced is doubtful but they are thought to have appeared in the early 1930s in both Australia and Europe.

The variety of Pieds would undoubtedly be the most popular of all the mutations. There were several appearances recorded prior to the establishment of the known varieties of today. The first Recessive Pied cock made its appearance in Copenhagen in 1932. This variety of Pied found its way into Australia in recent times and has become very popular.

In Sydney, in 1935, a Dominant Pied Green cock was exhibited at the Royal Zoological Society show. This bird was green, with half-yellow wings and a yellow bar across the chest. It also carried a round yellow spot on the back of the head. It is believed that this bird is the ancestor of all the Dominant Australian Pieds in the world today.

In Melbourne, at the Elizabeth Street markets one morning in 1935, Mrs S. Harrison of Murrumbeena, walked up to a bird dealer's stall. Looking up to a cage she noticed a green bird of unusual colouring. The cheek patch was of a different colour and she remarked that it also had jet-black tail feathers. Mrs Harrison purchased this bird for the sum of two shillings. Taking it home she later paired it to a Sky Blue and from this mating the first Dominant Grey bird was bred. These birds were the ancestors of all the Dominant Grey varieties in the world today.

The Yellow Face mutation appeared in England in 1937. About this time a Yellow-face with a much deeper facial colouring appeared in aviaries in Sydney. Today, this feature is often displayed prominently on birds of violet colouring.

There is no doubt that the appearance of the Longflight in 1938 has given the exhibition budgerigar of today some of its outstanding qualities. The ancestors responsible for this were discovered in an English village in 1941. They were all aviary bred Sky Blues and were 254 mm (10 in) long. Some of these birds were later secured for ten shillings each and they are the ancestors of most of the prominent English exhibition budgerigars of today.

It took more than thirty years for another prominent mutation to occur. This was the Spangle, which first appeared in Victoria around 1972. M. Jones, of Traralgon, Victoria, has since established this new mutation.

A dream for many fanciers and one that was discussed in 1933 in the English *Cage Bird's Annual* is the idea of producing a black budgerigar. The possibility of a break-through in this regards seems less remote now that the Spangle mutation has shown a reversal of the distribution of the markings on the feathers. For example, recently I saw on a Blue Spangle a wing that was completely black. This was dramatic evidence of complete pigmentation taking control over the whole wing.

Still, it is difficult to be really optimistic in this regard because the genes controlling body colour and markings are independent of each other. In the Opaline the colour of some markings takes on the same colour as the body colour, but so far no mutation has been produced where the process is reversed. Nevertheless, it is feasible that the opposite to a Clearwing can be produced, that is, a bird showing completely black wings and markings. Future breeding experiments will show if this control can be maintained and it is certain that they will be watched with great interest.

Budgerigars with obvious pink and red colouring have appeared on two separate occasions in Australia since 1945. Both cases were authentically recognised as true colouring and were used in breeding. In an outer suburb of Melbourne, Mr Ron Jones bred about a dozen birds with decidedly pink colouring. The colouring was evident on the body and the top of the head of Sky Blues and Cobalts. An official from the Budgerigar Council of Victoria advised Mr Jones on how to pair the birds in order to improve the pink colouring, and on his next visit the official was able to report that the numbers had increased to twenty, and on some the colour had improved to a brick red.

About this time there appeared newspaper stories of black and pink budgerigars being bred. These stories were accompanied by photographs and it appeared that the birds had been dyed. Mr Jones rang a Melbourne newspaper to advise them that he had been the first to breed pink budgerigars and, a story was printed in which, unfortunately,

the birds' existence and whereabouts were disclosed. Soon after this, Mr Jones stayed away from his residence overnight, leaving it unattended. On his return next day he found that all the birds had been stolen and that even eggs that were incubating were squashed in the nest. Police investigations revealed no trace of the birds and to date there has been no known re-occurrence of any such birds.

The second discovery was made by the late Sid French while walking in a Sydney suburb. He noticed an Albino with a large red spot on its head. The bird was a pet in a small cage and he approached the owners who, after a short conversation, revealed that they had bred the bird themselves in a small colony aviary.

They gave him this bird and the supposed parents, a Blue/Albino cock and an Albino hen. He paired these birds and made many other pairings later with the red-spotted Albino. None of the progeny showed any indication of red colouring. One morning in disgust Sid took the red-spotted Albino outside and threw it in the air. He never saw it again and he concluded that it was only a sport and would never reproduce the visual red pigment.

The appearance of other mutations and the combination of different forms have created only a passing interest. Novelties appear, creating a public interest whenever the unfortunate specimens, looking like feather dusters or mops, are put on display. In most instances these freaks of nature are neither welcomed or wanted by breeders, but are continually sought for financial gain.

Although not a mutation, the development of a strain of homing (free flying) budgerigars is often commenced from one specific bird. This enthusiastic enterprise is carried out widely by breeders in the United States.

The achievement of hybridising took place in Moree, in New South Wales, in 1963 and the credit goes to A. Menchin. The four hybrids were obtained from a Red Rump or grass parrot male x Lutino budgerigar female. On maturity their size was similar to a Bourke Parrot, which is much larger than a budgerigar. The offspring were creamy-yellow with orange displayed prominently on the rump: no head or wing markings were evident. All hybrids lived for approximately twelve months.

In summary, it is the chance that one may produce something different, perhaps even a new mutation, which makes breeding budgerigars so interesting and challenging and, if one is lucky, so rewarding.

Normal Light Green cock.

Albino cock.

Lutino cock.

Greywing Sky Blue cock.

14 THE LAWS OF INHERITANCE

Those who commence to breed by purchasing pure lines of birds learn very little genetically from the production of their young. Most backyard breeders, on the other hand, usually have birds from various sources, many of which have unknown pedigrees. As a result, they are likely to find colours and varieties of all descriptions in their nest boxes, none of which are visually representative of either parent. It is from results like these that the amateur will be led to seek answers to the question — Why is this so? Such an enquiring mind is a vital prerequisite to the understanding of the phenomena of reproduction.

The purpose of this section, then, is to explain as simply as possible the genetics of budgerigars. This will enable you to formulate possible results prior to the pair breeding, or after the actual reproduction of their offspring. The basic principles of inheritance in all forms of life were first formulated from experiments carried out on the humble garden pea. These principles, the Mendel Theory, carry the surname of their discoverer, Gregor Mendel (1822–1884). The results of his experiments were neglected and were not made known to the world until 1900, when his theories of heredity began to be fully appreciated. It was due to them that the breeding of plants and animals came to be placed on a scientific basis.

Mendel determined these principles by proving that in all germ cells (gametes) of a true breeding pea, there was a factor determining tallness. Similarly, in the gametes of the true breeding dwarf pea there was a factor determining dwarfness. Yet, when these two peas were crossed, only the tall character became visible. It became clear that the tall character was *dominant* and the factor for dwarfness could not be seen, and was therefore *recessive*. However, in turn, these tall peas produced, from the cross inherited in their gametes, not only a factor to produce tallness, but also the factor to produce dwarfness: the tall specimens of this first generation cross are known as *F1 hybrids*. When these F1 hybrids were crossed with each other they produced four individuals in this *mendelian ratio*: 1 pure tall dominant, 2 tall carrying the recessive factor to produce dwarfness, and 1 pure dwarf. This progeny of the second generation cross are *F2 hybrids*.

Mendel proved the laws of gamete segregation with the results of his F2 hybrids with their ratio of 3 to 1 — three tall to one dwarf — thus also proving that the various factors concerned are independent of each other, that is, the factor of tallness is segregated from the factor of dwarfness.

Reproduction

The reproduction cell in a female, the ovum, is penetrated by the male reproduction cell, the sperm, and conception takes place. Two partners are required in the reproduction process and they each contribute half of their hereditary factors. These factors, which have been handed down from generation to generation, are transmitted in the genes. The genes are carried on the chromosomes, like beads on pieces of string. The chromosomes occur in pairs and both male and female each contribute one half to all newly formed pairs that determine the sex and colour of the individuals, as well as other physical and hidden factors of each.

Sex determination

The sex of a bird is determined at the time the egg is fertilised. Both the cock and the hen inherit two chromosomes. Cocks carry the XX combination; hens the XY combination.

A hen's eggs will carry, in approximately equal numbers, either the X or the Y chromosome. When a sperm carrying X fertilises an egg carrying X the result will be an XX combination: a cock. When a sperm carrying X fertilises an egg carrying Y the results will be an XY combination: a hen. In this way the sex of the young are determined by the hen.

Sex-linkage

The term 'sex-linked' is often regarded as something completely mysterious. The varieties of budgerigar that are sex-linked are the Opaline, Cinnamonwing, Lutino, Albino and Lacewing, all of which manifest this inbuilt characteristic, which can be transmitted, depending on the matings, in a form that is visual or in a form that is invisible. Sex-linkage is irrevocably tied to the male producing chromosomes (the X chromosome) in both the cock and the hen bird and thus is transmitted, together with the sex determining factor, directly into the germ cell during reproduction.

With this knowledge, we can accurately predict the varieties of offspring. A cock bird has two X chromosomes and a hen bird has one. A Lutino cock must have the Lutino factor linked with both of its chromosomes. The Lutino hen has to have the Lutino factor linked to its X chromosome too. A cock bird that is split for the Lutino factor carries it in only one of its two X chromosomes, and as such, the bird is not visually a Lutino. On the other hand, because hens have only one X chromosome they cannot be split for this Lutino factor.

We should now see that there are five possible combinations where sex-linkage is involved. They are:
1 Lutino cock — factor visible.
2 Split Lutino cock — factor not visible.
3 Non Lutino cock — has no Lutino factor.
4 Lutino hen — factor visible.
5 Non Lutino hen — has no Lutino factor.

Table 1 (right) is an outline of the expectations that can occur if any one of the cock birds 1, 2 or 3 is mated with either hen 4 or 5. No other possibilities exist.

Definition of the word 'split'
The term 'factor not visible' is expressed as a split.

Thus, when a particular bird is said to be split a certain variety or colour, it means that this individual has inherited powers to reproduce that variety or colour when suitably paired over a number of matings. In a breeder's terminology the visible character is always stated first and the hidden character is stated after. The diagonal stroke (/) is the symbol which represents the word split. Thus, a bird normally referred to as Green split Blue will be represented as Green/Blue.

Colour

People who see the domesticated budgerigar today must wonder if they are the same colour in the wild. Many may also wonder if the budgerigar has always been the same colour in the wild as they are

Table 1 Sex-linkage expectations where the sex-linked birds are Lutinos.

Note: Non sex-linked birds used in the tables are Normals.

1 Lutino cock x Lutino hen
  Expectation: 100% Lutino cocks and hens
2 Lutino cock x Normal hen
  Expectation: 50% Normal/Lutino cocks
              50% Lutino hens
3 Normal cock x Lutino hen
  Expectation: 50% Normal/Lutino cocks
              50% Normal hens
4 Normal/Lutino cock x Lutino hen
  Expectation: 25% Lutino cocks
              25% Lutino hens
              25% Normal/Lutino cocks
              25% Normal hens
5 Normal/Lutino cock x Normal hen
  Expectation: 25% Lutino hens
              25% Normal/Lutino cocks
              25% Normal cocks
              25% Normal hens

Reproduction of two sex-linked varieties
The progeny that can be expected when two sex-linked varieties such as Cinnamonwings and Opalines are combined is illustrated by the following matings.

today. If we follow Charles Darwin's theory it is quite possible that they may have changed colour since their beginning in order to survive the environmental changes that have taken place.

In terms of breeding, and the possibilities of colour production in parrot life, the budgerigar is a forerunner. It is an excellent introduction to the range of pigmentation available for the interested breeder to aspire to. With the information available on this topic it would be difficult to predict what colours may eventually be produced in the budgerigar.

To produce existing and new colour varieties of budgerigar it is essential to know the true value and nature of colour and to understand the breeding principles governing the factors of heredity. Only then can one hope to reproduce the colour one is seeking. The breeders who trust to chance may find that many of their efforts will end in failure.

Budgerigars are divided into colour groups of green, yellow, blue and white. The plumage colour

1st mating:
Cinnamon cock x Opaline hen
Expectation: Normal/Cinnamon/Opaline cocks
                 Cinnamon hens

2nd mating:
Normal/Cinnamon/Opaline cock x Cinnamon hen
Expectation: Normal cocks. All /Cinnamon
                 50% /Opaline

                 Cinnamon cocks
                 50% /Opaline

                 Normal hens
                 Cinnamon hens
                 Opaline hens
                 Cinnamon Opaline hens

3rd mating:
Normal/Cinnamon/Opaline cock x Cinnamon Opaline
hen
Expectation: Normal cocks. All /Cinnamon and
                 /Opaline
                 Cinnamon cocks
                 50% /Opaline

                 Opaline cocks
                 50% /Cinnamon

                 Cinnamon Opaline cocks

                 Normal hens
                 Cinnamon hens
                 Opaline hens
                 Cinnamon Opaline hens

is a result of colouring pigments carried to the feather by the blood. Thus, it is important to realise that any colour can be created from existing colour combinations in much the same way as one would mix similar colour pigments in paint.

Scientific research programmes on the budgerigar's colour factors were undertaken independently by two geneticists Dr Duncker and Dr Steiner. Although a considerable amount of time has passed since the inception of their theories, their results still form the basis for determining the pigmentation of the separate colours and the factors regulating their distribution.

It has been proven that the appearance of a green budgerigar is due to the combination of three pigments, yellow (lipochrome), black (eumelanin) and brown (phaeomelanin). Consequently, when the dark pigments of black and brown are not present, the result is a yellow budgerigar. On the other hand, the absence of the yellow pigment will result in a blue bird and if a bird does not have the ability to develop pigmentation and is unable to display any colour in its plumage it is a white bird. With the removal of the brown pigment the result is a grey-green bird; with the removal of the brown and yellow pigment we can produce a grey bird.

With the removal of the black pigmentation, eumelanin, from a bird's markings a variety of birds with brown or cinnamon markings displayed in place of the black markings is possible. Moreover, there is also an altered factor which produces abnormal reddish, yellow or brownish eumelanin through which the varieties of Fallows appear: this affects the colour of the eye, changing it from black to red.

The absence of oxidation in the pigmentation inhibits the expression of the inherited melanins and gives rise to the Lutino and Albino. These individuals also have the pigmentation reduced from the eye, which is red.

In addition, there is a separate regulating factor controlling the melanistic colour factor present in the wing and zebra markings, tail feathers and throat spots. Quite obvious signs of its presence within the markings is in the wing colour on Greywings in any Blue series. The lightly coloured wing would resemble a dirty white, the medium coloured wing would be the correct shade of grey (half-way between black and white), and the dark wing would be almost black.

Green and blue body colours come in shades which range from light to dark. These colour characteristics, with their hereditary factors are classified below:

Light	*Medium (intermediate)*	*Dark*
No dark factor	1 dark factor	2 dark factors
Light green	Laurel (dark green)	Olive
Sky	Violet and Cobalt	Mauve

The Grey, Yellow and White factor birds all appear in the three gradations.

Within all body colours, as well as in the wing and body markings, there is a melanin factor which controls the depth of colour. This is of the utmost importance in the production of regulated colour and one can never obtain a medium shade, let alone a dark shade, if one pairs two light-shaded birds.

It should be stressed here too, that the body colours and wing markings are independently controlled. This is quite obvious, for example, where a Greywing of excellent body colour (dark shade) possesses a poor or light coloured (light shade) wing.

The Cheek Patch

The cheek patch may, at times, look rather unimpressive but it holds the key to the first obvious signs of melanin in the body colour, that is, the dark colour factor. This feature was first observed by very early breeders of new mutations. The variation in the colour of the cheek patch was quite visible in the Green where it was indigo, in the Yellow where it was mauve, and in the Blue where it was violet. This has proved beyond doubt that the cheek patch colour was linked with the body colour. It is even more obvious now in the Dominant Grey factor birds whose cheek patches are various shades of bluish-grey.

Thus, in the early days of breeding budgerigars, it must have appeared to be only a matter of time before birds of light, medium and dark colouring would be produced once the variations of cheek patch colour were observed. Thus, the violet colouring of the cheek patch was a sign that a violet coloured bird would eventually make an appearance.

Genetic types

The following explanations refer to the use of pure Normal Green and Blue birds as shown in Figure 13.1.

Genotypes: This group contains individuals whose genetic constitutions are made up of a known group of factors. For example, in Figure 13.1, **1** and **2** represent two different colour genotypes, each of which has a definite hereditary constitution.

Phenotypes: These are a class of individuals whose outside appearance does not give any sign or clue to their genetic makeup, for example, **3** and **4** in Figure 13.1 — in the breeders' terminology: Green/Blue.

Mendel showed that inheritance followed certain

Figure 13.1
Illustration of the establishment of a pure line and propagation of a mutation.

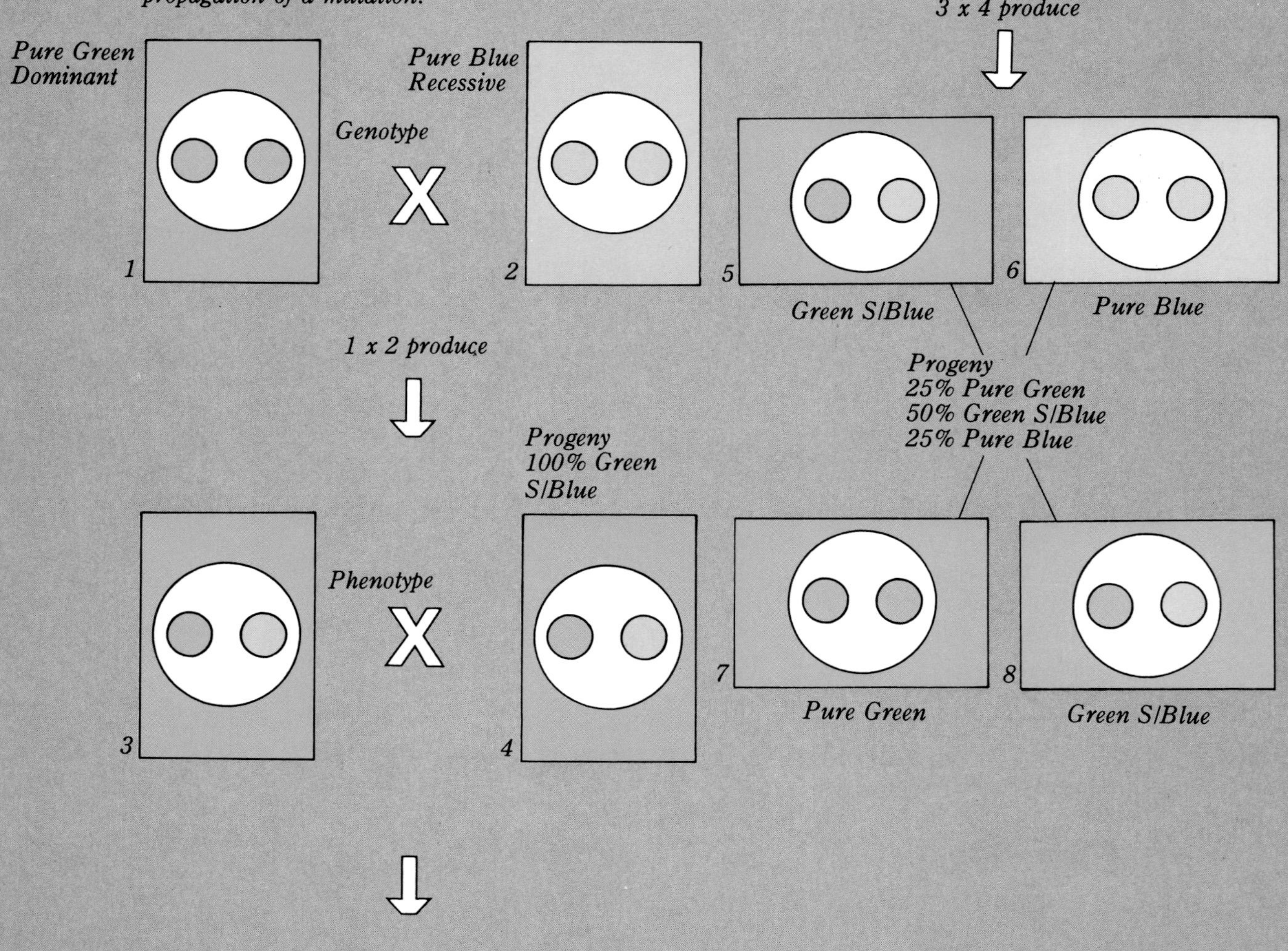

Pure Green Dominant

Pure Blue Recessive

Genotype

1

2

3 x 4 produce

Green S/Blue 5

Pure Blue 6

1 x 2 produce

Progeny 100% Green S/Blue

Phenotype

3

4

Progeny
25% Pure Green
50% Green S/Blue
25% Pure Blue

Pure Green 7

Green S/Blue 8

ordered principles and Figure 13.1 aims, in the simplest way possible, to show the formula for these principles, which apply even to the most complex combinations.

In breeding, dominance may be partial or complete: complete dominance in colour is referred to as *pure*; and complete dominance in variety is referred to as *double factor*. The only truly complete dominants are the Dutch Pied, Australian Pied, Grey, Yellow-face (Type 2) and the new mutation of Spangle. Nevertheless, to produce 100 per cent of their kind, these birds must possess the double factor. When a single factor is present only half will be visibly exhibiting their kind.

Partial Dominance

When a bird inherits a pair of dissimilar genes the variety or colour is determined by the dominant gene because its characteristics are visible. The recessive

gene remains invisible. Thus in Figure 13.1, a Green (1) and a Blue (2) are paired to produce (3) and (4), which are Green/Blue. Their offspring express the Green gene which is dominant and the recessive Blue gene is carried hidden.

When (3) and (4) were paired they produced (7), a pure Green; (5) and (8) partial dominant Green/Blue; and the recessive in this case was (6), the Blue series bird. Now when one crosses (5), partial dominant Green/Blue with (6), the recessive Blue, one produces (9), partial dominant Green/Blue and (10), the recessive Blue. Then by pairing (6) and (10), one gets 100 per cent pure Blue progeny, whose progeny in turn become the genotype of pure Blue, (2).

Recessive factors

The highly complex explanation of the main recessive factors is best made with the use of Normal birds, which keep these factors hidden.

Explanation of Dominant Normals
Normals exist in various colours and shades of green and blue. They still retain the original Wild Green's black feathers on the wing, and the zebra and spot markings. The edges of these feathers (ground colour) are yellow in the Green bird and white in the Blue bird. In all individual Normals there is no variation in body colour or markings.

To include the Blue bird will only complicate the simplicity of Figure 13.2 because, as was shown in Figure 13.1, the Blue bird is recessive to Green. In addition, Blue also belongs to Form 2 (see below), that is, it can be produced from a pairing of a Green/Blue and a Green/White because White is recessive to Blue.

Explanation of recessive change
Recessives, such as the Greywing, Clearwing and Fallow (Figure 13.2) can be produced in all the body colours of Normals, however, when this occurs the black colour on the wings and in the markings changes or disappears completely. In addition, these recessive genes are in no way sex-linked.

Explanation of recessive characters
In budgerigars the three forms of the recessive factor are not always visual. The fact that the recessive characters may be hidden, that is, in split form, does not mean that they are not there and, if two partners with recessive factors are mated, the youngsters produced will vary according to the statistical rules in Figure 13.1.

5 Green S/Blue   X   6 Pure Blue

5 x 6 produce

Progeny
50% Green
S/Blue
50% Pure
Blue

9   10

Progeny
100% Pure
Blue

6 Pure Blue   X   10 Pure Blue

Form 1

In this form two partners carrying the same recessive factor are necessary in order for reproduction to take place. They will then superimpose their recessive factor on most colours and varieties in accordance with the orders of inheritance. Examples of this form in Australia are the Recessive Pied and the Recessive Fallow. This form of recessive character is reproduced in the same manner as the Sky Blue in Figure 13.1.

Form 2

These recessive factors show degrees of dominance over each other and it is not always necessary to mate with the same factor in order for reproduction to take place.

Form 3

A cock with a double dose of the cinnamon gene and a hen with a single dose of the cinnamon gene should normally exhibit the inherited cinnamon plumage. But, when two recessive factors for melanin suppression are present, the cinnamon quality will be suppressed visually, either partially or completely. The varieties and colours that possess this double character are termed a duplex combination — they are the Greywing, Clearwing, Yellow and White.

A budgerigar's outward colour does not necessarily give a true indication of its inheritance. When we deal with the five recessive factors shown in Figure 13.2 one will soon realise their complicated character. But first, in order to understand recessive factors, it is necessary to arrange them in their melanistic (colour) suppression order.

It must also be remembered that any regulated colour pigmentation can visually express itself in progressively diminishing degrees. A further point is that because the markings and the body colour factors are controlled independently of each other, this colour reduction of a bird's plumage may take place only in the markings or only in the body.

Recessives in Figure 13.2

Order of dominance simply corresponds to the amount of pigmentation expressed — that is the greater the pigmentation the greater the dominance.

Our recessive order begins with the Greywing. This factor, (B) in Figure 13.2, is a result of a reduction in the distribution of the darker colour formations (melanins) causing the markings to be lighter in colour.

Next down the table is the Clearwing (C) in which there is a further decrease of the darker pigmentation in the markings. When we proceed to the Black-eyed Yellow (D), the reduction of all the melanin produces a bird that is without markings and whose entire plumage is the basic colour yellow. Then with the Black-eyed White (E), all the pigmentation has been suppressed. At the very bottom of the table is the Fallow (F), which although not a true colour variety, has a genetic structure that enables it to be mated with any of the four characters above, thus creating the double dose needed for the appearance of any one of the above characters.

Explanation of Figure 13.2

Figure 13.2 is dominated by Normal Green (A). For each variety a list is given of the recessive factors each individual may inherit in their order of recessiveness. In each group the evidence of split character may not always be the result of a specific attribute in either of the parents, but rather the product of a combination of the dominant recessive with any one of the represented lower recessive characters.

Figure 13.2 shows us that one pair of Greens (A) can give us Greywings, Clearwings, Yellows, Whites and Fallows. The pair of Greywings (B) may also give Clearwings, Yellows, Whites and Fallows. The pair of Clearwings (C) may produce Yellows, Whites and Fallows. While the pair of Yellows (D) may only give us Whites and Fallows and the Whites (E) can only give us Fallow Whites. However, within the groups any type of bird may be mated with a type of bird below it in the order of recessiveness to produce the type of the dominant, for example, Clearwing (C) may be mated with the Yellow (D) or the White (E) or the Fallow (F) to produce a Clearwing precisely similar in appearance although its reproduction powers are concealed and unknown.

Remember, however, this systematic approach can only proceed down until we have reached the White. The White bird, if appearing as a Fallow White hen, is therefore, genetically pure both for variety and colour.

The reproduction of all recessive factors in budgerigars is governed and controlled by the laws of heredity as shown by the reproduction of the genotype of the recessive colour blue in Figure 13.1.

	COCKS			HENS	
1	**A. NORMAL GREEN**			**A. NORMAL GREEN**	
	Latent Characters			Latent Characters	
	/ Greywing	(B)		/ Greywing	(B)
	/ Clearwing	(C)		/ Clearwing	(C)
	/*B-E Yellow	(D)		/*B-E Yellow	(D)
	/*B-E White	(E)		/*B-E White	(E)
	/ Fallow	(F)		/ Fallow	(F)
2	**B. GREYWING**			**B. GREYWING**	
	Latent Characters			Latent Characters	
	/ Clearwing	(C)		/ Clearwing	(C)
	/*B-E Yellow	(D)		/*B-E Yellow	(D)
	/*B-E White	(E)		/*B-E White	(E)
	/ Fallow	(F)		/ Fallow	(F)
3	**C. CLEARWING**			**C. CLEARWING**	
	Latent Characters			Latent Characters	
	/*B-E Yellow	(D)		/*B-E Yellow	(D)
	/*B-E White	(E)		/*B-E White	(E)
	/ Fallow	(F)		/ Fallow	(F)
4	**D. *B-E YELLOW**			**D. *B-E YELLOW**	
	Latent Characters			Latent Characters	
	/*B-E White	(E)		/*B-E White	(E)
	/ Fallow	(F)		/ Fallow	(F)
5	**E. *B-E WHITE**			**E. *B-E WHITE**	
	Latent Character			Latent Character	
	/ Fallow	(F)		/ Fallow	(F)

Figure 13.2   ***Black-eyed**

Table of recessive expectations
1 Recessive x Recessive
Expectation: 100 per cent Recessive
2 Recessive x Dominant/Recessive
Expectation: 50% Recessive
50% Dominant Recessive
3 Dominant/Recessive x Dominant/Recessive
Expectation: 25% Recessive
50% Dominant/Recessive
25% Dominant
4 Recessive x Dominant
Expectation: 100% Dominant/Recessive
5 Dominant/Recessive x Dominant
Expectation: 50% Dominant
50% Dominant/Recessive

The laws of inheritance are very complex but, whatever your breeding aim, time spent in gaining some knowledge of them will be time well spent. For specific information and further insight into the budgerigar's complicated genetic structure, the book *Budgerigar Matings and Colour Expectations*, published by The Budgerigar Society of England, is very useful. Not only does it explain most theories, but it also discusses over 2 000 different matings.

Australian Dominant Pied cock in a U.K. aviary.

The perfect wing of a Spangle.

Two outstanding cock birds belonging to a prominent English fancier.

An exceptional Light Green hen bred by one of England's top lady breeders.

15 METHODS FOR BREEDING VARIETIES AND COLOURS

Many people who keep a few pairs of budgerigars just for pleasure often perform, what is to them, experimental breeding. And, in spite of a lack of knowledge of breeding techniques and the difficulties involved, many manage to combine common-sense and flair to obtain good results. Using the simplest methods they learn of some of the varieties and colours that can be produced from certain specimens.

The basic principles of inheritance are explained in the chapter, Laws of Inheritance. In this chapter a less complicated form of reproduction is outlined and matings to breed certain individuals are given. Nevertheless, it should be remembered that a budgerigar's visible character is revealed by the colour of its plumage, and its hereditary constitution is carried hidden in the genes.

The simplest breeding method for the reproduction of a particular variety or colour is accomplished by selecting a parent that shows the characteristic one is seeking. This parent will, to some extent, transmit the variety or colour required to its young. If the young do not show the visible character desired, a back-cross with father to daughter or mother to son will be necessary over a number of matings, thus enabling its kind to be reproduced. In simple terms a back-cross is a mating performed with the aim of transmitting factors that are concealed in one or both parents to the offspring of the cross.

The following explanations regarding the production of certain colours and varieties are very basic and the specialist breeder may on occasion possess a strain of birds with some minor modification which will cause them to produce slightly different results.

Individual body colours

Body colour is bred in the same manner in all varieties of budgerigar mentioned in this chapter. Bad colour cannot be expected to pass on good colour to their progeny, therefore it is necessary to introduce good body colour. It should also be understood that some colours suffer from being paired indiscriminately to other forms; for example,

a green bird paired to a yellow bird will produce greens with very diluted body colour.

When an effort is made to produce birds which closely resemble any given colour, it is important that we should have some idea of their mode of inheritance. Within the colour groups of greens and blues we have individual groups of light, medium and dark body colours. The bird that is visually yellow will also be masking the colour green in any one of the three forms: that is, light, medium and dark. Moreover when correctly mated, it will be capable of reproducing the shade of green. Similarly, the white bird has the capacity to reproduce whatever shades of blue are inherited in its makeup.

For convenience then, and for quick referral, a systematic list of the various colour matings, together with their expected results, is outlined below. And, if one wishes to deviate from the suggested matings outlined later, one will be able to form some idea of what can be expected.

Colour expectation table

Parents	Results (Per cent)
1 Light x Light	100 Lights
2 Light x Medium	50 Lights
	50 Mediums
3 Light x Dark	100 Mediums
4 Medium x Medium	25 Light
	50 Medium
	25 Dark
5 Medium x Dark	50 Medium
	50 Dark
6 Dark x Dark	100 Dark

Although the above table may be quite simple when applied to birds of blue colouring, when the dominant colour of green is introduced in the form of a green/blue, the offspring produced will be exactly fifty per cent greens and fifty per cent blues over a large number of pairings.

Genetic types

When the semi-dominant dark green gene made its

existence known it was given the name, Dark Green. The use of these birds when they are split for Blue often brings unexpected results because of the cross-over in their genetic types, therefore the following explanation may be necessary.

Laurel

The Dark Green, as it is referred to in most countries, is commonly known to most Australians as a Laurel. In my opinion, the latter label is preferable because the colour of this bird is really only a medium or intermediate shade of green.

Provided they are split for Blue or White, any Laurel, or medium or intermediate Grey-Green, or Yellow, can be either a Type 1 or a Type 2. For example, take the Laurel Green. If you pair an Olive to a Sky, the Laurels produced from this pairing will be Type 1, because they will have received the dark factor from a bird of green colouring. If you then pair a Laurel (Type 1) with a Sky Blue, the theoretical expectation will be 43 per cent Laurel/Blue (Type 1), 43 per cent Sky Blue, 7 per cent Light Green/Blue and 7 per cent Cobalt.

On the other hand, if you pair a Light Green to the darkest Blue (mauve) you will produce Laurels (Type 2) because they will have received the dark factor from a bird of blue colouring. These Laurels (Type 2) will produce the complete opposite to the Type 1 when paired to a Sky Blue. The expectations from this pairing will be 43 per cent Light Green/Blue, 43 per cent Cobalt, 7 per cent Laurel/Blue (Type 1) and 7 per cent Sky Blue. Thus, the Laurels produced in the above pairing have reverted back to Type 1 because their dark factor has been inherited from a green parent.

When a Laurel (Type 1) is paired to a Mauve, 43 per cent will be Olive/Blue, 43 per cent Cobalt, 7 per cent Laurel/Blue (Type 2) and 7 per cent Mauve. When a Laurel (Type 2) is paired to a Mauve the result is the complete opposite again: 43 per cent Mauve, 43 per cent Laurel/Blue (Type 2), 7 per cent Olive/Blue and 7 per cent Cobalt.

Within the Green and Blue series birds there are three groups: the light group — Light Green and Sky Blue; the medium group — Laurel, Cobalt and Violet; the dark group — Olive and Mauve. Grey and Violet, which are able to superimpose their colouring over any green and blue bird will be dealt with separately.

Breeding separate colours

Light Green

The reproduction of the colour, Light Green, requires at least one green or yellow parent of light or medium colouring. If the breeding of Light Green in numbers is your sole objective then the mating of Light Green x Light Green would prove the best method. For the breeder specialising in this colour the above mating may be satisfactory also, but only if the colour of the stock is above average.

Where the Green's body colour has become faded and patchy, mating of Light Green x Sky Blue is especially profitable, if the Sky Blue is a good colour. The pairing of a Light Green to a Laurel is not recommended because, in most cases, this could have a detrimental effect on both colours. On the other hand, the cross Laurel/Blue (Type 2) x Sky Blue will produce a good Light Green. It will also produce a larger percentage of Light Greens and Cobalts.

Laurel

The colour of Laurel can be reproduced with the use of at least one medium or dark green or yellow bird. The best method for their production in numbers is: Light Green x Olive, Sky Blue x Olive, or Light Green x Mauve. For the specialist breeder the preferred matings are Olive x Cobalt, Laurel/ Blue (Type 1) x Sky Blue and Laurel x Olive. Within these matings extreme variations in body colour will often occur as the depth of the laurel increases.

Olive

The colour of Olive can only be reproduced from the use of a green or yellow parent of medium or dark colour. If you wish to produce them in numbers the mating of Olive x Olive and Olive x Mauve will give you all Olive birds. For the specialist breeder, these matings are also successful, although the Olives should be the darkest procurable and preference should be given to those showing an evenness of colour (not patchy) on the lower part of the body.

Excellent results are often produced also from the mating of Olive x Cobalt, especially when the Cobalt is a good even colour.

Sky Blue

The colour of Sky Blue can be reproduced with Green/Blue, Yellow/White and also blue and white birds of light or medium colouring. Whenever Sky Blues are to be bred in numbers the mating Sky Blue x Sky Blue will produce all Sky Blues. For the specialist breeder this pairing is successful when one or both partners excels in colour.

Excellent results can also be obtained from mating Light Green/Blue x Light Green/Blue or Light Green/Blue x Sky Blue. In addition the pairing of Laurel/Blue (Type 1) x Sky Blue will produce the larger percentage of Laurel/Blue (Type 1) and Sky Blues.

Cobalt

The Cobalt can be reproduced with the use of at least one Green/Blue, Yellow/White, or a blue or white medium or dark coloured bird. Whenever you wish to produce Cobalts only the mating Sky Blue x Mauve will produce all Cobalts.

For the specialist breeder, this is undoubtedly one of the hardest colours to reproduce and matings that include a double dose of the dark factor gene generally give the best results. The matings of Olive/Blue x Sky, Olive/Blue x Cobalt, and even Laurel/Blue (Type 1) x Olive/Blue should yield good results.

Mauve

The colour of Mauve can be reproduced with a Green/Blue, Yellow/White, and blue or white of medium or dark colour. When Mauves only are desired the mating Mauve x Mauve will produce all Mauves. The specialist breeder has little choice other than the selected pairing of Olive/Blue x Olive/Blue or Laurel/Blue (Type 2) x Olive/Blue and Olive/Blue x Mauve. The pairing you choose will depend on the characters available with deep and even colour.

Grey factor birds

The colour known as the Australian Grey is a dominant factor and its characteristics will alter the tone of all green and blue birds. Greens will become Grey-greens, Blues will become Greys, Yellows will become Grey-yellows and Whites will become Grey-whites. Whenever one wishes to reproduce these birds a grey factor parent will be necessary.

Grey factor birds also have light, medium and dark shades, although sometimes it may be difficult to discern which shade of grey a bird represents. For example, it may not be clear whether a particular bird is a good deep light shade, or a bad dark shade. If the true identity is not established unsuitable pairings will result. Thus, only the breeder who knows his or her family of grey factor birds well should use them to help reproduce good colour in any green or blue bird. On the whole, however, the colour grey tends to reduce colour rather than enhance it.

Grey-green

The production of these birds in quantity is best achieved from the mating Grey-green x Grey-green. When the specialist is pairing for colour a medium to light colour parent would be advisable if birds of medium colour are desired. Crosses such as Grey-green x Grey and Grey-green x Sky Blue or Cobalt also produce good results. The appearance of light greeny-yellow in a Grey-green bird is undesirable.

Grey

The best results for their production in numbers occurs when pairing Grey x Grey. When the specialist breeder undertakes their breeding, the grey that is a medium colour is generally the most attractive, especially when accompanied by a nice white mask and facial area. This bird could result from the matings: Grey-green/Blue x Grey, any Laurel/Blue x Grey, or Grey x Sky Blue, Cobalt or Mauve: all would prove good pairings provided they possessed good even body colour.

Violet

The violet factor is dominant, and is inherited quite independently of any other characters. Visual Violets are simply a variation of the Cobalt, and are a medium colour. The character violet is in fact a colour modifier that often acts in the same manner as the grey factor, that is, by imposing its presence over other colours. Although there are often instances where Violets are produced from birds that do not express any visual proof of its existence, the dominant violet factor cannot be carried in any split form. In such instances, therefore, the appearance of Violets is due to the poor colour of the parents. A bird with the violet factor in the light, medium or dark colours is described in the genetic table in this manner: Green plus Violet or Sky Blue plus Violet. However, in ordinary discussion they are freely referred to as Violet Light Greens and Violet Skys etc.

The most promising cross to produce Violets is the mating, Sky Blue plus Violet x Mauve plus Violet: at least half of the young produced should be Violets. From the mating, Violet x Violet six colours are produced: Sky Blue, Sky Blue plus Violet, Cobalt, Violet, Mauve, and Mauve plus Violet. Such Violet birds mated into the whole green colour range will yield excellent colour in both green and blue birds, for example, the best Light Green I have ever seen was produced from the mating Light Green/Blue x Sky plus Violet.

To produce good coloured Laurels the mating Olive plus Violet/Blue is excellent. Successful breeding of Olives occur from the crosses Olive plus Violet/Blue x Olive and Olive x Mauve plus Violet. Excellent Sky Blues are produced from Light Green plus Violet/Blue x Sky Blue and Cobalts and Mauve of good deep even colour can result from the mating Violet x Violet.

At most times the violet factor becomes quite distinguishable in specimens of good colour, even Grey-greens and Greys. Sometimes, however, its presence may only be detected by an inspection of the two main tail feathers. Generally, however, these will not appear to be different to those normally seen on any light, medium or dark green or blue bird.

In conclusion, the presence of the violet factor tends to be more of an advantage than a disadvantage because, when correctly controlled, it will enhance not only the body colour but also the depth in the colours in the markings.

Normals

The Normal with its black markings is the most numerous of all budgerigars and is closest in appearance to its wild ancestor. The body colour is represented in all the previous colour forms mentioned but the colour of the markings is dominant and cannot be carried hidden, except in a Lutino and Albino. For the breeder who wishes to breed Normals the mating Normal x Normal would be ideal.

For the specialist breeder wishing to increase stamina and introduce other desirable features outcrosses into both Opaline and Cinnamon are advisable.

Opaline

The variety of Opaline has a sex-linked character. With its variations in the inherited black markings it is readily combined with most other varieties and colours to produce an attractive specimen. For the breeder who wishes to reproduce Opalines, the cross Opaline x Opaline will result in 100 per cent of their kind. In a mating where only an Opaline cock is used (Opaline cock x Normal hen) the daughters only will all be Opalines.

The specialist breeder often uses the opaline factor in a combination to produce many high class specimens, particularly Cinnamons. There are two types of Opalines: the clear back, and the specimen heavily marked in the area of the 'V' and the mantle. The latter should be avoided, especially

A bold-headed Grey-Green cock, reputed to be one of the best in the U.K.

Top quality English budgerigars.

when pairing to a Normal for outbreeding to effect an improvement to the Opaline.

Yellow-face

This character is very striking particularly on any Blue or White series individual and combination with it is sought by most breeders.

There are two types of Yellow which have been bred from two separate mutations, the one, the Cream Face (Type 1), and the other with its exceptional yellow features (Type 2) which is prominent in Australia. Both types can be present on any bird, although they will not be obvious on

Green or Yellow series birds, and both types have a dominant character although the Type 1, when in the form of a double factor (producing 100 per cent of their kind), may occur without the apparent Yellow-face colouring; that is, reverting to ordinary white-faced birds.

The best method of producing the variety in numbers is always Yellow-face x Yellow-face and any breeder wishing to specialise in this variety will have to continually select individuals without the obvious yellow ground colour which often persists in the wing markings.

First outcrosses to blue or white birds some-

The evidence of an English breeder's skill becomes apparent by the control of the pied markings on each bird.

A matched pair of Cinnamonwings with two of their offspring in an English aviary.

times reproduce characters with noticeably green body colour. This fault will only be rectified with the continual back-crossing to Yellow-faced Blue or White birds without this superficial character. Type 1 breeders do not encounter these obvious body colour problems, however, the continual selection of individuals with yellow faces of the deepest colour will always be necessary.

Yellows

The colour of Yellow, which normally appears as a Black-eyed Yellow, can be bred from the yellow factor received from a green or yellow bird. For the breeder who wishes to breed all Yellows the mating Yellow x Yellow or Yellow x White will yield 100 per cent Yellows.

For the specialist breeder, the method of selecting the two deepest coloured specimens, with at least one individual with clear yellow wings, would be desirable. However, when we proceed into outcrosses and combine the improvement of colour and the elimination of markings, we will encounter many variations in this lengthy programme. The yellow bird represented in the colour plate is the product of many years of selection and intermating. This bird is also a combination of two characters, Yellow and Cinnamon, although we cannot recognise the presence of Cinnamon at this stage of her life. Also the bird cannot yet be distinguished as being light, medium or dark.

When one attempts an outcross for any particular reason, one does not wish to encounter more problems than is necessary and experience shows that a knowledge of the colours of the partners in the experiment is essential. For this reason the use of birds displaying or carrying hidden Lutino, Albino or Greywing factors should be avoided. The influence of light, medium and dark (olive yellow) colours should only be encountered in the early back-crosses when we are endeavouring to expel their body suffusion. Although the Grey-green has proven to be one of the best outcrosses, we will see the influence of the grey in a dull sheen on the body colour and a heavy greyish-yellow colour on the rump. For this reason the grey factor is best eliminated when one has secured the desired improvement. This is achieved by the simple method of detecting and selecting individuals which do not display the greyish tone in the cheek patch.

Emphasis throughout this process should be laid upon the importance of good colour and the Cinnamon and the Opaline varieties can be used to add clearness and depth to colour in Yellows because their features are detectable and controllable.

While the colour programme has been in progress, we should also have been mating individuals to clear the dark pigmentation from the often pronounced markings.

The possession of the cinnamon gene is essential in the production of good Yellows because of the suppression of the pigmentation in the markings. Clearwing and Yellows are two factors for its melanin suppression. The foundation of any good strain of Yellows is developed from specimens obtained from Clearwing, split Yellow or White matings that yield heavily suffused Yellows or Whites. Some of these young will also possess the cinnamon gene through which we will eventually see the emergence of the self-coloured Yellow. By continually selecting the clearest characters to the deepest coloured Yellow partners you should obtain a fair number of young showing the good points of their parents. And by this gradual process the cultivation of good Yellows are obtained.

Black-eyed Whites

Black-eyed Whites can be obtained by using the same process used to produce Yellows, although the preferred pairings would be with birds of grey or yellow colouring. Generally, however, the dark melanin will always come to expression on the markings, thus making it more difficult to breed a clear specimen.

There are, also, Dark-eyed Clear Yellows and Whites. These result from complicated matings between the Dutch and Recessive Pied. However, because the mutation of Spangle has appeared on the scene and appears to perform the same process, it is possible that we may eventually see completely new yellow and white birds.

Lutino

The red-eyed sex-linked character Lutino is the common yellow bird we see. However, hidden under its cloak can be a green or yellow bird of any description. For the person who requires only Lutinos the mating Lutino x Lutino will always produce all Lutino young.

For the specialist breeder, one can take note of the results of the late Billy Hoare, who was a leader in this field. He advised that in breeding Lutinos there are two features to avoid: suffusion of colour and visible markings. It is obviously futile to combine the latter factor with the Lutino factor. If we do not adhere to this advice a form of Lacewing will eventually appear.

The Lutino gene causes the melanins to appear in a pale form, therefore to be able to produce the effect of good colour there must be present in the Lutino plumage a double dose of the dark factor (Olive). When we combine this with one whose ground colour is abnormally yellow (Yellow-face Type 2) the result should be perfection in colour.

Whenever one brings outcrosses into these sex-linked forms the use of a hen mated to a Lutino cock is preferable, if the mating is reversed a year will be lost because no visual Lutinos will appear. The means of selecting these outcrosses is of the utmost importance. The important key is to select an Olive of deep even colour in order to obtain colour intensity in the body. The Yellow-face of a double factor in the form of a Mauve, with the obvious presence of strong yellow ground colour, will determine the colour effect required in the flight feather.

This process continues by avoiding birds with light flight feathers and selecting Lutinos that exhibit deep yellow masks and plumage colour free from green body suffusion. Upon this strict observance the development of superior specimens should then come into existence.

Albino

The result of albinism of any blue or white bird is the red-eyed sex-linked white bird. For production in numbers the mating Albino x Albino will provide the best possible results. In the opinion of many, the most attractive is the Yellow-faced Albino. The yellow face is introduced by the mating of an Albino cock x any Yellow-faced Blue or Grey hen. All hens from this pairing will be Albinos and a percentage should display the yellow face.

To the breeder who wishes to produce their own Albinos from Lutinos, the crossing of two Lutino cocks with blue or grey hens will be needed. If Albinos are not present in the resulting progeny, which is only possible when the Lutinos are split White, then inter-mating of the progeny in the next season should yield a one in four result.

For the specialist breeder body suffusion is often a problem that can be eliminated by crosses and back-crosses with grey factor birds, for example, an Opaline Greywing Grey hen.

Greywings

The colour of Greywings can be produced without the visual evidence of its presence from the mating of two Normal/Greywing birds. However, unlike the Normal, the Greywings markings can be present on a pure Yellow or White budgerigar.

Whenever one's sole object is to breed Greywings, whatever the colour or variety, the mating Greywing x Greywing is always the preferred pairing. Another good mating is Greywing x split Greywing which results in fifty per cent Greywings and fifty per cent splits. If you cross Greywing Yellows with a Yellow or White you could produce Greywing Yellows or Yellows only, because a Yellow or White cannot be split for Greywing.

For the specialist breeder, it is not advisable to pair a Greywing and a Clearwing because the blending of these two recessive characters will tend to reduce the colour of the markings.

Also, with the cross Greywing Green x Yellow the body colour of all Greywing Green/Yellow produced will be a greeny-yellow. However, if one wishes to persist with such split Yellow birds, the mating of /Yellow x Cinnamonwing Yellow will, after many years of careful selection, result in the much admired Greywing Yellow.

Clearwings

These beautiful yellow- or white-winged budgerigars can be produced from the mating of two Normal/Clearwing birds but they are undoubtedly the hardest variety to reproduce. Therefore, Clearwing x Clearwing should always be your preferred pairing.

The problem for the specialist breeder may be the presence of the greywing factor. Therefore, when a cross into Normals is undertaken, a test pairing of the intended individual with a yellow or white bird would always be advisable.

It is necessary when commencing a strain of Clearwing to incorporate the yellow or white factor in their production. Such birds will appear, at first, as heavily suffused Yellows or Whites in any of the light, medium or dark colours, however, their prominent feature will be the clearness of their wings. These birds should be back-crossed with the clearest and deepest coloured masked specimens for the eventual process of purity in the markings.

Cinnamons

The recessive sex-linked character, Cinnamon, can often be present in budgerigars even though it may not be visible. For example, the appearance of any pink-eyed young in the nest for the first week after birth is a sign that they are a Cinnamon carrier. When a cinnamon plumage is required a good deep

Cinnamon x Cinnamon is the desirable pairing.

For the specialist the problem arises in the maintenance of depth in the cinnamon markings. This intensity of colour can be developed by regular back-crossing into Normals with depth and clearness in their markings. Depth in the markings of a Cinnamonwing Yellow will only be oabtained by back-crossing into Dark Greywing Yellows to retain good yellow body colour.

Fallows

This so often forgotten variety exhibits the beautiful pastel shades in the Blue colourings. When these are combined with the Yellow-faced character we often see the loveliest of all the colour combinations. Fallows, of course, can be any colour or variety: their distinction is only in the reduction in the shade of their pigmentation. When we cross Fallow to Fallow we produce 100 per cent Fallows.

For the specialist breeder who wishes to increase the depth of colour, this can be achieved by back-crossing into good Normals. The best cross is split Fallow x split Fallow which, although it will only give us one Fallow in four, will produce a specimen that generally makes the exercise very worthwhile.

Pieds

There are many different Pied varieties but the two groups that concern us are Dominant and Recessive. It is possible to produce Pieds in all the colours and varieties although the pied areas will not be visible on any yellow or white bird.

In Pieds the pattern of distribution cannot be controlled accurately, although the variations, to a certain extent, can be applied from heredity by close breeding. Therefore, when you require special pied markings look for the desired pied areas and try to cultivate them by mating two similarly marked birds together. The form required may be obtained by the continual pairing of such specimens.

Dominant Pieds

The Australian and Dutch Dominant Pieds work in the same genetic reproduction pattern. From any mating with a double factor all pieds are breed. With two single factors the resulting progeny will be twenty-five per cent double factor Pieds, fifty per cent single factor Pieds and twenty-five per cent non Pieds. For the colony breeder, the breeding of Greywing Pieds, which are always attractive, may take two seasons. However, if either an Opaline or Cinnamonwing cock is crossed with a Pied hen, Opaline or Cinnamonwing

Pied hens may be produced in one year.

Recessive Pieds

Only in the Recessives will the mating of Pied x Pied always produce 100 per cent Pieds. These Recessive birds have a much brighter plumage colour than their Dominant counterparts. After the first cross of Pied x non Pied, which produces 100 per cent split Recessive Pieds the best mating to increase size is to back-cross one of these splits to a Recessive Pied: the progeny will be fifty per cent Recessives and fifty per cent non Pied splits. But to repeat the same breeding procedure using one of these fifty per cent non Pieds, or second generation splits, will only lead to inferior specimens being produced.

Using Dutch Dominant/Recessive Pied hen x Recessive Pied cock, a small percentage of dark-eyed Clear Yellow or White birds may be bred.

Spangle

We are all novices when it comes to the dominant variety of Spangle which imposes its character visually on any bird displaying markings. The most attractive individuals are the Spangle Cobalts and Violets. The mating of double factor Spangle (which appears as a suffused Yellow or White) x non Spangle will, theoretically, yield 100 per cent visual Spangles. For this reason, it is believed that this variety will have a great impact on the hereditary constitution of all budgerigars. For example, the mating of a Spangle and a non Spangle will result in non Spangle young of large size — this fact alone contradicts the opinion that mutations generally lack the stamina to reproduce size.

Combinations

The combination of separate colours and varieties often takes place when birds are colony bred, but to produce these combinations by controlled breeding is often a lengthy process. Combinations such as Yellow-faced Greys or Cinnamonwing Pieds are readily seen but others, such as Yellow-faced Opaline Clearwing Blues (Rainbows), are not a common occurrence.

The practical breeder must realise that in order to produce any combination one must first secure the varieties and colours responsible for its appearance. Then, after studying their orders of dominance over each other, a plan can be devised for the quickest method for their eventual appearance.

Winning Grand Champion, after a successful breeding season for the author.

NOTES

Introduction

1 Neville W. Cayley, *Budgerigars in Bush and Aviary,* Angus and Robertson Ltd, Sydney, 1933.

Chapter 2   The Budgerigar and its Natural Environment

1 D. Thomson, Life with the Bindibu-9, *Daily Telegraph,* 10 March 1958. Professor Thomson was then Associate Professor of Anthropology, Melbourne University.

2 M. Wilson, Birds in the Simpson Desert, *Melopsittacus undulatus, Emu,* vol. 74, 1974, p.174.

3 T. J. Cade and J. A. Dybas Jr, Water Economy of the Budgerigar, *Auk,* 79, 1962, pp. 345-64.

4 *Sydney Morning Herald,* 11 October 1962.

5 Budgies just Nomads, *Sun Herald,* 22 June 1975.

6 CSIRO Division of Wildlife Research, Australian Bird-banding Scheme. Mr David Purchase, who administers this scheme, advised me that with the co-operation of Dr E. Wyndam approximately 1,000 budgerigars were banded in western New South Wales. Unfortunately, however, no bands were returned to help determine any of the bird's movements.

7 MacGillvary, Notes, *Emu,* vol. 29, 1929, p. 121.

8 *Bulletin,* 9 March 1932.

9 J. Neil McGilip, *S.A.Ornithologist,* vol. 11, 1931, pp. 11, 12.

10 *The Advertiser,* Adelaide, 27 January 1932.

11 *The News,* Adelaide, 6 February 1932.

12 *Bulletin,* 2 March 1932.

13 *The Advertiser,* Adelaide, 2 May 1932.

14 *Daily Telegraph,* 19 December 1974.

Chapter 3   The Budgerigar as a Pet

1 Karl Russ, *The Speaking Parrot,* L. Upcott Gill, London, pp. 251-2.

2 John Gould, *Handbook to the Birds of Australia,* vol. 2, London, 1865, p. 82.

Chapter 13   Mutations

1 D. Shillings, *Emu,* vol. 48, 1948.

GLOSSARY

Back-cross: A mating performed so that some of the offspring will show unmistakeably the hereditary constitution of both partners.

Barred heads: A term used for youngsters in baby plumage whereby the barrings are extended close to the cere.

Barrings: Lines of zebra marked feathers on cheeks, neck and head.

Birdroom: A building where birds are to be confined in any number of cages for various reasons.

Bloodline: A strain that has been developed by a particular breeder.

Bloom: The ultimate finish on the feather that brings about sheen.

Breeding season: Period of time in which birds are mated to reproduce.

Chromosomes: Bodies present in the cell.

Chromosome – X and Y: These differ in the male and female. The male has two X chromosomes and the female has one X and one Y.

Club rung birds: Birds that wear a closed aluminium leg band stamped with an individual number, club and year issue number. This enables the recorded identification by both the owner and the issuing club concerned.

Cobbier bird: Short and thick.

Colony breeding: Uncontrolled breeding in an aviary.

Colour: A bird's colour depicts its classification.

Controlled breeding: The selection and housing of individual pairs.

Crop: The commencement of the digestive tract.

Culling: Process of visual examination whereby birds not reaching your required standard are rejected.

Dark Gene: This has the power to present its influence in two forms. Single dose; i.e. Laurels and Cobalts. Double dose; Olives and Mauves.

Dominant: A factor that will express itself at the expense of others.

Double dose: This is a requirement for the appearance of a particular character.

Down: A soft fluffiness noticeable on growing chicks.

Egg binding: Inability of a hen to pass the egg.

Factor – double: The inheritance of the same factor from both parents.

Factor – single: The inheritance of a factor from only one parent.

Fancier: One who enjoys the hobby of birdkeeping.

Flights: An area enabling the birds freedom for exercise.

French Moult: A disease that creates an unnatural shedding of the feathers prior to or after the youngsters leave the nest.

Germ cells: The reproductive cell produced from the merging of the spermatozoon of the male and the ova by the female.

Grit: Finely broken down shell and sand.

Ground colour: Its natural presence as either yellow or white.

Hikers: Birds suffering from French Moult and unable to fly.

Hybrids: Offspring produced from the inter-mating of different species.

Melanins: The separate inheritable colour pigments.

Moult: A gradual process whereby the old feathers drop out and new ones grow.

Mutation: This occurs when genes do not follow the normal pattern. The result is a bird not previously seen.

Nest feather: A bird in pre-adult plumage.

Outcross: The inter-mating of unrelated individuals often in respect to colour or variety, to develop a bird's physical and genetic constitution.

Parishes Food (Hepasol): A tonic based on Syrup of Glycerine Phosphate.

Pigmentation: Colouring of the feather.

Progeny: Offspring from a breeding pair.

Quill: The main shaft of a feather.

Recessive: A factor that submerges itself at the expense of others.

Runners: Refer hikers.

Self-coloured: Clear colour with no evidence of markings.

Specialist breeder: Specialises in breeding a particular colour or variety.

Splayed legs: Deformed legs spread outwards.

Split: A bird carrying a factor hidden.

Sport: A bird that is incapable of reproducing its visual character.

Standard of perfection: Pictorial model.

Trainer or training cage: Small cages used in quieting birds prior to exhibiting.

Unbroken caps: Refer barred heads.

Variety: This is determined by the bird colour or other visual expressions that change its appearance.

Vent: Anus.

Yellow, buff and double-buff feathers: Terms used to describe a particular type of feather structure.

Zebra markings: Wavy markings.

INDEX